Researching Education Through Actor-Netw

Educational Philosophy and Theory Special Issue Book Series

Series Editor: Michael A. Peters

The *Educational Philosophy and Theory* journal publishes articles concerned with all aspects of educational philosophy. Their themed special issues are also available to buy in book format and cover subjects ranging from curriculum theory, educational administration, the politics of education, educational history, educational policy, and higher education.

Titles in the series include:

Researching Education Through Actor-Network Theory
Edited by Tara Fenwick and Richard Edwards

The Power In/Of Language
Edited by David R. Cole & Linda J. Graham

Educational Neuroscience: Initiatives and Emerging Issues
Edited by Kathryn E. Patten and Stephen R. Campbell

Rancière, Public Education and the Taming of Democracy
Edited by Maarten Simons and Jan Masschelein

Thinking Education Through Alain Badiou
Edited by Kent den Heyer

Toleration, Respect and Recognition in Education
Edited by Mitja Sardoč

Gramsci and Educational Thought
Edited by Peter Mayo

Patriotism and Citizenship Education
Edited by Bruce Haynes

Exploring Education Through Phenomenology: Diverse Approaches
Edited by Gloria Dall'Alba

Academic Writing, Philosophy and Genre
Edited by Michael A. Peters

Complexity Theory and the Philosophy of Education
Edited by Mark Mason

Critical Thinking and Learning
Edited by Mark Mason

Philosophy of Early Childhood Education: Transforming Narratives
Edited by Sandy Farquhar and Peter Fitzsimons

The Learning Society from the Perspective of Governmentality
Edited by Jan Masschelein, Maarten Simons, Ulrich Bröckling and Ludwig Pongratz

Citizenship, Inclusion and Democracy: A Symposium on Iris Marion Young
Edited by Mitja Sardoc

Postfoundationalist Themes In The Philosophy of Education: Festschrift for James D. Marshall
Edited by Paul Smeyers and Michael A. Peters

Music Education for the New Millennium: Theory and Practice Futures for Music Teaching and Learning
Edited by David Lines

Critical Pedagogy and Race
Edited by Zeus Leonardo

Derrida, Deconstruction and Education: Ethics of Pedagogy and Research
Edited by Peter Pericles Trifonas and Michael A. Peters

Researching Education Through Actor-Network Theory

Edited by

Tara Fenwick and Richard Edwards

WILEY-BLACKWELL

A John Wiley & Sons, Ltd., Publication

This edition first published 2012

Chapters © 2012 The Authors

Book compilation © 2012 Philosophy of Education Society of Australasia

Originally published as a special issue of *Educational Philosophy and Theory* (Volume 43, Supplement 1)

Blackwell Publishing was acquired by John Wiley & Sons in February 2007. Blackwell's publishing program has been merged with Wiley's global Scientific, Technical, and Medical business to form Wiley-Blackwell.

Registered Office

John Wiley & Sons Ltd, The Atrium, Southern Gate, Chichester, West Sussex, PO19 8SQ, United Kingdom

Editorial Offices

350 Main Street, Malden, MA 02148-5020, USA

9600 Garsington Road, Oxford, OX4 2DQ, UK

The Atrium, Southern Gate, Chichester, West Sussex, PO19 8SQ, UK

For details of our global editorial offices, for customer services, and for information about how to apply for permission to reuse the copyright material in this book please see our website at www.wiley.com/wiley-blackwell.

The right of Tara Fenwick and Richard Edwards to be identified as the authors of the editorial material in this work has been asserted in accordance with the UK Copyright, Designs and Patents Act 1988.

Wiley also publishes its books in a variety of electronic formats. Some content that appears in print may not be available in electronic books.

Designations used by companies to distinguish their products are often claimed as trademarks. All brand names and product names used in this book are trade names, service marks, trademarks or registered trademarks of their respective owners. The publisher is not associated with any product or vendor mentioned in this book. This publication is designed to provide accurate and authoritative information in regard to the subject matter covered. It is sold on the understanding that the publisher is not engaged in rendering professional services. If professional advice or other expert assistance is required, the services of a competent professional should be sought.

Library of Congress Cataloging-in-Publication Data

Researching education through actor-network theory / edited by Tara Fenwick and Richard Edwards.
     p. cm.
   Includes bibliographical references and index.
   ISBN 978-1-118-27489-7 (pbk.)
   1. Education–Research–Methodology.   2. Actor-network theory.   I. Fenwick, Tara J.
II. Edwards, Richard, 1956 July 2–
   LB1028.R384 2012
   370.72–dc23

                                                                    2012001068

A catalogue record for this book is available from the British Library.

Cover image by www.cyandesign.co.uk

Set in 10/13 Plantin by Toppan Best-set Premedia Limited
Printed in Malaysia by Ho Printing (M) Sdn Bhd

1   2012

Contents

Notes on Contributors

Richard Edwards is Professor of Education and Head of the School of Education, University of Stirling. His published work has focused on issues of spatiality and materiality in education, curriculum and literacy, educational policy, and lifelong learning more broadly. Email: richard.edwards@stir.ac.uk

Tara Fenwick is Professor of Professional Education at the School of Education, University of Stirling. Her research currently focuses on professional knowledge, practice and education in the workplace, with particular interest in sociomaterial theory. She has published widely in theories of workplace learning. Email: tara.fenwick@stir.ac.uk

Radhika Gorur is a Research Fellow at the University of Melbourne. Her research interests include education policy, evidence-based policy, and material semiotic theories. She is particularly interested in following the practices of measurement of performance and equity in education. Email: gorurr@unimelb.edu.au.

Mary Hamilton is Professor of Adult Learning and Literacy in the Department of Educational Research, Lancaster University, UK and Associate Director of the Lancaster Literacy Research Centre. She researches, publishes and teaches in the field of Literacy Studies, discourse, policy and change. Email: m.hamilton@lancaster.ac.uk

Dianne Mulcahy is a Senior Lecturer in the Melbourne Graduate School of Education at the University of Melbourne. Her published work in Education concerns policy and political issues surrounding educators' professional formation and development. Her recent research activity has centred on capturing the complexity of educators' professional learning, with particular attention to the materiality of this learning. Email: monicadm@unimelb.edu.au

Jan Nespor is a professor at The Ohio State University. An educational anthropologist, he has published works on curriculum and learning in higher education, urban elementary schooling, the politics of computer-mediated instruction in universities, qualitative methodology, and other topics. Email: nespor.2@osu.edu

Foreword

Actor-network theory (ANT) insists on forms of nonhuman agency and focuses on how networks get formed. As a form of material-semiotics, it emerges in science studies and is faithful to the ethnomethodological school and consonant with poststructuralist and constructivist commitments. It is particularly useful in analyzing large technical systems. Already there is enough in this brief encapsulated description to challenge the ontological commitments and epistemological orientations of most social science approaches and to recommend the adoption of the approach to educationalists. Tracing its origin meanings to Diderot Bruno Latour (1998) writes: 'Put too simply ANT is a change of metaphors to describe essences: instead of surfaces one gets filaments (or rhyzomes in Deleuze's parlance) (Deleuze and Guattari, 1980). More precisely it is a change of topology. Instead of thinking in terms of surfaces—two dimension—or spheres—three dimension—one is asked to think in terms of nodes that have as many dimensions as they have connections'.[1]

In *Researching Education Through Actor-Network Theory*, Tara Fenwick and Richard Edwards both renew and reclaim actor-network theory for educational research demonstrating its potential and power in a series of related papers selected and edited for their insights into educational processes. This is an authoritative collection by experts in the field who as editors and contributors provide the basis for a good understanding and application of actor-network theory in educational research.

Michael A. Peters
University of Waikato, NZ

---

[1] See "On actor network theory: A few clarifications" at http://www.nettime.org/Lists-Archives/nettime-l-9801/msg00019.html.

Introduction

Tara Fenwick & Richard Edwards

Actor-network theory (ANT) continues to enjoy a lively trajectory in the social sciences since its emergence in the early 1980s at the Centre de Sociologie de l'Innovation (CSI) of the École nationale supérieure des mines de Paris. Largely associated with its progenitors in science and technology studies (STS) including Bruno Latour, John Law and Michael Callon, ANT has contributed an important series of analytic approaches and considerations that rupture certain central assumptions about knowledge, subjectivity, the real and the social. The focus is on the socio-material—and how minute relations among objects bring about the world. Analyses drawing upon ANT trace how different human and nonhuman entities come to be assembled, to associate and exercise force, and to persist or decline over time. Nothing is given or anterior, including 'the human', 'the social', 'subjectivity', 'mind', 'the local', 'structures' and other categories common in educational analyses. Throughout the 1980s and 1990s, ANT figured prominently in studies published in sociology, technology, feminism, cultural geography, organization and management, environmental planning and health care. With a few limited exceptions, however, educational research in the main has not demonstrated a similar enthusiasm in the uptake of ANT.

We are among those who believe that ANT offers truly important insights about the processes and objects of education. This is in spite of, or actually partly because of, its mutations in the past two decades into a highly diffuse, diverse and contested set of framings and practices. Its own key commentators refuse to call it a 'theory' as though ANT were some coherent explanatory device. It may be more accurate to think of ANT as a virtual 'cloud', continually moving, shrinking and stretching, dissolving in any attempt to grasp it firmly. ANT is not 'applied' like a theoretical technology, but is more like a sensibility, a way to sense and draw (nearer to) a phenomenon. For educational researchers, as we argue in Fenwick and Edwards (2010) and Fenwick *et al.* (2011), ANT's language can open new questions and its approaches can sense phenomena in rich ways that discern the difficult ambivalences, messes, multiplicities and contradictions that are embedded in so many educational issues.

This book is an experiment, intended to engage readers in the question: What work can ANT do in educational research? To bring some focus to the book, we called for chapters addressing issues of educational change or reform. The authors employ a range of ANT constructs to explore and perform educational change in highly diverse manifestations: integration of new technology, a large-scale school improvement initiative, everyday curriculum enactments, development of international standardized tests, introduction of teacher evaluation systems and implementation of a literacy program. Each author argues for the unique analysis that ANT approaches enable, yielding overall an important expansion of how we engage with educational change. While one objective of each chapter is to show an ANT sensibility at work with a particular researcher in a particular environment of concerns, each also focuses, as ANT studies are expected to do, on tracing the rich material details of the actual actors and their story being followed by the researcher. The remainder of this introduction outlines ANT for educators, as described in Fenwick and Edwards (2010), for those who may be.

About Actor-Network Theory

The risk in explaining ANT is distorting and domesticating it. Its ideas are practices for understanding, not a totalizing theory of the world and its problems. Jan Nespor puts it well in his chapter when he describes ANT ideas as 'ontological acids undermining reductive explanations and pushing us towards engagements with evidence'. The more well-known ANT ideas that authors have taken up are described here briefly, including symmetry, translation, network ontology, network effects, (im)mutable mobiles, obligatory points of passage and scale play. We also introduce selected critiques of ANT and certain 'after-ANT' conceptions such as multiple ontologies. We hope to avoid the trap of re-establishing and imposing a purity of ANT-ness that Law (1999, p. 10) has warned of: 'Only dead theories and dead practices celebrate their identity'.

ANT examines the interconnections of human and nonhuman entities based upon an anti-foundationalist approach in which nothing exists prior to its performance or enactment. Human intention and action are therefore decentred in this approach. The objective is to understand how these things come together—and manage to hold together—to assemble collectives or 'networks' that produce force and other effects: knowledge, identities, routines, behaviours, policies, curricula, innovations, oppressions, reforms, illnesses and on and on. ANT thus helps us to ask: What are the different kinds of connections and associations created among things? What different kinds and qualities of networks are produced through these connections? What different ends are served through these networks? A key assumption is that humans are not treated any differently from nonhumans in ANT analyses. This assumption, elaborated by Bruno Latour (1987), is called 'symmetry'. Everyday objects and parts of objects, memories, intentions, technologies, bacteria, texts, furniture, bodies, chemicals, plants ... all things are assumed to be capable of exerting force and joining together, changing and being changed by each other. The networks thus formed can keep expanding to extend across broad spaces, long distances or time periods. Of course, networks can also break down, or dissolve, or become abandoned. ANT analyses show how things are attracted into or excluded from these networks, how some linkages work and others do not, and how connections are bolstered to make themselves stable and durable by linking to other networks and things. In particular, ANT analyses focus on the minute negotiations that go on at the points of connection. Things persuade, coerce, seduce, resist and compromise each other as they come together. They may connect with other things in ways that gather them into a particular collective, or they may pretend to connect, partially connect or feel disconnected and excluded even when they are connected.

Latour (1999) fights any ontological separation between materiality and meaning as a rupture between the thing and its sign that are part of each object. He considers a central problem to be the 'circulating reference' between words and world that attempts to transform matter, the objects of knowledge, into representations, as though there were justifiable *a priori* distinctions between mind/matter or object/sign. He, like Ian Hacking (2000) and Deborah Barad (2007), is therefore critical of social constructivists as well as realists in assuming that materiality and representation are separate realms. The important point is that ANT focuses not on what texts and other objects mean, but on what they do. And what they do is always in connection with other human and nonhuman things. Some of these connections link together to form an identifiable entity or assemblage, which is referred to as an 'actor' that can exert force. 'Playground', for example, represents a continuous collaboration of bats and balls, swing installations, fences, grassy hills, sand pits, children's bodies and their capacities, game discourses, supervisory gazes, safety rules and so on. This playground is both a moving assemblage or network of things that have become connected in a particular way, and an actor that can produce fears, policies, pedagogies, forms of play and resistances to these forms—hence, actor-network. And the objects that have become part of this actor-network are themselves effects, produced by particular interactions with one another.

ANT analyses try to faithfully trace all of these negotiations and their effects. In the process, they show how the entities that we commonly work with in educational research—classrooms, teaching, students, knowledge generation, curriculum, policy, standardized testing, inequities, school reform—are in fact assemblies or gatherings of myriad things that order and govern educational practices. Yet, these assemblies are often precarious networks that require a great deal of ongoing work to sustain their linkages. So, such analyses can show how such assemblages can be unmade as well as made, and how counter-networks or alternative forms and spaces take shape and develop strength. The focus is on how things are enacted rather than attempting to explain why they are the way they are.

Those familiar with ANT debates will know that many speak of 'after-ANT' or 'post-ANT'. Some avoid using explicit ANT terminology, characterizing their work as complexity, socio-materiality, material semiotics or STS. The frustration expressed by the most prominent ANT commentators is that many early ANT studies reified concepts such as networks, solidified particular models of analysis and colonized their objects of inquiry in representational ways that ANT approaches were intended to disrupt. A landmark volume of essays entitled *Actor Network Theory and After* (Law, 1999) was premised on the assumption that ANT ideas proliferating throughout the 1990s had largely run into an impasse. At that time, Law (1999), for example, was worried that ANT's topological assumptions had come to homogenize the possibilities of understanding complexity in spatial and relational socio-material events. Other authors, representing leading scholars associated with ANT at that time, declared various approaches forward that included eliminating or replacing certain naturalized ANT language and models, delimiting ANT's claims and opening its conceptual scope.

At the time of this writing, 13 years on from the publication of *Actor Network Theory and After*, there has been a remarkable profusion of ANT studies, critiques and hybrid theoretical blends as ANT has travelled across disciplines ranging from feminist technology studies to cyberpunk semiotics to environmental activism. Some authors have argued for ANT's particular value in educational research (e.g. see Edwards, 2002; Nespor, 2002; McGregor, 2004; Waltz, 2006; Harmon, 2007; Mulcahy, 2007; Fenwick & Edwards, 2010). These explorations have each helped to extend and reconfigure ANT ideas, opening challenging questions and ways of thinking for educational researchers. We believe that it is more helpful to use one term 'actor-network theory' to refer to this constellation of ideas that have associated themselves with 'ANT' at some point, rather than to attempt problematic periodizations of early-ANT, after-ANT, ANT-diaspora and so forth. We employ ANT as a marker—understood to be a contingent and conflicted signifier—for approaches that share notions of symmetry, network broadly conceived, and translation in multiple and shifting formulations.

Translation—How Change Occurs

In some early formulations, ANT has been described as a 'sociology of translation'. Translation is the term used by Latour (1987) to describe what happens when entities, human and nonhuman, come together and connect, changing one other to form links. At each of these connections, one entity has worked upon another to translate or change it to become part of a network of coordinated things and actions. 'Entity' is a loose way to refer to various things that can be human and nonhuman, including different kinds of material objects and immaterial (conceptual, moral, virtual) objects and actions, that are not pre-given, essentialized and defined. As Law (1999) tries to explain, an entity is more than one and less than many, not a multiplicity of bits nor a plurality, a division into two or more others. In traditional ANT language, while the working entity is called an 'actor', the worked-upon entity is referred to as an 'actant'. In other words according to Latour (1999, p. 18), when the actant becomes translated to become a performing part of the network, the actant behaves with what appears to be particular intentions, morals, even consciousness and subjectivity. In other words, when translation has succeeded, the entity that is being worked upon is mobilised to assume a particular role and perform knowledge in a particular way. It performs as an actor.

Translation is neither deterministic nor linear, for what entities do when they come together is probable but unpredictable. They negotiate their connections, using persuasion, force, mechanical logic, seduction, resistance, pretence and subterfuge. Connections take different forms, some more elastic, tenuous or long-lasting than others. Translations may be incremental, or delayed across space and time. Entities may only peripherally allow themselves to be translated by the network. In Latour's (2005) ontology, entities undergo myriad negotiations throughout the process of translation. For Harmon (2007), this is an important contribution of ANT to education: tracing exactly how entities are not just effects of their interactions with others, but are also always acting on others, subjugating others and making things possible. All are fragile, and all are powerful, held in balance with their interactions. None is inherently strong or weak, but only becomes strong by assembling other allies.

Eventually these dynamic attempts by actors to translate one another can appear to become stabilized: the network can settle into a stable process or object that maintains itself. Like a black box, it appears naturalized, purified, immutable and inevitable, while concealing all the negotiations that brought it into existence. Examples would be a mandated list of teaching competencies, or an 'evidence-based' educational practice accepted as 'gold standard'. Each entity also belongs to other networks in which it is called to act differently, taking on different shapes and capacities. A teaching contract, for example, is a technology that embeds knowledge, both from networks that produced it and networks that have established its use, possibilities and constraints. In any employment arrangement, the contract can be ignored, manipulated in various ways or ascribed different forms of power. Thus, no agent or knowledge has an essential existence outside a given network: nothing is given in the order of things, but performs itself into existence. And however stable and entrenched it may appear, no network is immutable. Counter-networks are constantly springing up to challenge existing networks. Continuous effort is required to hold networks together, to bolster the breakages and to counter the subterfuges.

Networks

If translation is what happens at the nodes of a network, where one entity successfully acts upon another, how does a network actually grow? One suggestion was offered in ANT's early years by Callon (1986), in a much-cited and critiqued conception of networks assembling and extending themselves through 'moments' of translation. The critiques have centred on problematic applications of Callon's ideas as a fixed model, which tends to distort the complexity it was intended to liberate. This is undoubtedly as true in educational research as it has been in other fields of social science. However, there also exist educational studies showing the utility of Callon's moments of translation in illuminating how some networks become so durable and apparently powerful in education, exerting influence across far-flung geographic spaces and time periods. Callon (1986) proposed that some types of network begin with problematisation where something tries to establish itself as an 'obligatory passage point' that frames an idea, intermediary or problem and related entities in particular ways. The translations whereby separate entities are somehow attracted or invited to this framing and where they negotiate their connection and role in the emerging network Callon called interessement, which not only selects those entities to be included but also importantly those to be excluded. Those entities to be included experience enrolment in the network relations, the process whereby they become engaged in new identities and behaviours and increasingly translated in particular directions. When the network becomes sufficiently durable, its translations are extended to other locations and domains through a process of mobilisation.

In ANT terms, a network is an assemblage or gathering of materials brought together and linked through processes of translation, that together perform a particular enactment. A textbook or an educational article, for example, each bring together, frame, select and freeze in one form a whole series of meetings, voices, explorations, conflicts, possibilities explored and discarded. Yet these inscriptions appear seamless and given, concealing the many negotiations of the network that produced it. And a textbook or article can circulate across vast spaces and times, gathering allies, shaping thoughts and actions and thus creating new networks. The more allies and connections, the stronger the network becomes. Law (1999, p. 7) explains that in a network 'elements retain their spatial integrity by virtue of their position in a set of links or relations. Object integrity, then is not about a volume within a large Euclidean volume. It is rather about holding patterns of links stable'.

ANT's network ontology is particularly useful for enabling rich analyses of contexts, which have become increasingly important in educational analyses of pedagogy, curriculum and educational change (Edwards *et al.*, 2009). Contexts such as schools, lecture halls and workplaces are created and continually shaped through social and material processes. These folds and overlaps of practises are very much about network relations. In fact, human geographers have long worked with ANT, using its ideas, critiquing and extending them, to understand social space as a multiplicity of entities engaged in fluid, simultaneous, multiple networks of relations (see Murdoch, 2006, for a review). Power is central to any understanding of space and context as produced through networks of socio-material relations. ANT analyses can also trace how assemblages may solidify certain relations of power in ways that continue to affect movements and identities. For example, the sedimentation of power relations in educational spaces and their continuing effects are ubiquitous. Nespor's (1994) oft-cited study of the differences in social behaviour and curricula between physics and business students at a university examines the ways that architecture interacts with particular codified knowledge to order flows of action, people and objects, constituting space in fundamentally different ways.

In ANT's early years, the notion of network was employed to suggest both flow and clear points of connection among the heterogeneous entities that became assembled to perform particular practices and processes. However, with the proliferation of technological network systems and the ubiquity of the network metaphor to represent such phenomena as globalization and social capital, the term has problematically suggested flat linear chains, enclosed pipelines and ossified tracks. Frankham (2006) points out how educators have particular reason for caution when networks are everywhere invoked to represent idealized learning communities that are homogenous and a-political. ANT-associated writings have explored alternate metaphors of regions and fluid spaces (Mol & Law, 1994) to approach the complexity of socio-material events and avoid imposing a linear network model on the ineffable and imminent. Some have explored ways of retaining notions of network by refusing pipeline associations and showing diverse shapes and forms that a network can assume. Some networks are provisional and divergent, while others are tightly ordered, stable and prescriptive.

One problem with this network conception is what and where one should focus in conducting educational research. Miettinen (1999) makes this point in his critique of ANT, arguing that the network ontology is infinite and therefore unworkable for researchers. Indeed 'cutting the network' (Strathern, 1996) has always been deemed a necessary aspect of using ANT in research, but being explicit about how that enacts the effects of research in certain ways. Wherever one marks boundaries around a particular phenomenon to trace its network relations, there is a danger of both privileging that network and rendering invisible its multiple supports. Critiques of ANT studies have noted their fondness for examining powerful, visible networks, and their tendency to reproduce network participants' views of their reality (Hassard *et al.*, 1999). Representations of networks are themselves concrete, implying the realities to be far more stable and durable than imminent, precarious shifting socio-material relations ever can be.

Familiar issues of reflexivity are no less problematic in ANT accounts, which can objectify networks as something produced solely in the eye of the researcher, and simultaneously forget to paint the researcher's representations into the portrayal of network translations, thereby leaving the entire analysis in control of the researchers. This not only turns a supposedly heterogeneous, symmetrical perspective into a decidedly human-centred one, but also pretends to honour uncertainty and messiness in what is in effect a predetermined account. In choosing a focus for study, ANT researchers confront McLean and Hassard's (2004, p. 516) challenge:

> ... to produce accounts that are sophisticated yet robust enough to negate the twin charges of symmetrical absence or symmetrical absurdity [and] to understand the paradoxical situations in which ANT researchers find themselves in conducting field studies and producing accounts, notably in respect of notions of power, orderings and distributions.

This is what the contributors to this book have attempted.

Effects of Networks—Agency, Power, Identity and Knowledge

The overriding insight of ANT views of the world is that all objects, as well as all persons, knowledge and locations, are relational effects. The teacher is an effect of the timetable that places her in a particular room with particular students, in a class designated as Social Studies 6, among textbooks, class plans and bulletin boards and stacks of graded papers with which she interacts, teaching ideas and readings she has accumulated in particular relationships that have emerged with this year's class of children. In the pedagogical practices of her work, she is a 'knowing location'. In one example, McGregor (2004, p. 366) traces how the teacher as knowing location is produced in Science classrooms through:

> ... the laboratory, with its electricity points, water and gas lines. The Bunsen burners and flasks set up by the technicians, who have also ordered and prepared the necessary chemicals according to the requisition sheet, the textbooks and worksheets that the students are using. Mobilized also are the teacher's experience and education.

These are further affected by networks of activity that composed and timetabled the student group in a particular way and allocated the teaching assistants. These things that act at a distance—buzzer, database, textbooks—are what Latour (1987) originally called immutable mobiles. Immutable mobiles are only visible within a particular network of relations. They can be silent, ignored or overridden by other active objects. However, they have developed enough solidity to be able to move about and still hold their relations in place. In effect, they function as the delegates of these other networks, extending their power by moving into different spaces and working to translate entities to behave in particular ways. Law and Singleton (2005) explain that whether an object is more or less abstract (a pedagogical idea compared to an instrument) is less the point, because the key feature is that it is identified, has material effects, in particular networks of historical, cultural, behavioural relations that make it visible.

But many immutable mobiles are not at all immutable: they break and shift, grow and adapt and mutate as they travel. Returning to the teacher as a knowing location, what of her agency and subjectivity? She is planning lessons, choosing particular pedagogical approaches, deciding whether to solve the myriad classroom problems that emerge in this way or that. How does ANT avoid casting her as determined and recognize her own force exercised through her pedagogical participation? How does ANT understand the sources and effects of her intentions, her desires and the meanings she makes of her pedagogical encounters with students? Certain critiques of ANT have accused it of failing to appreciate what is fundamentally human and subjective in flows of action, suggesting that perhaps it ought to modify its stance of radical symmetry to admit that humans are different because they make symbolic meaning of events and exert intentional action (Murdoch, 1998).

However, ANT's ontology of folding and unfolding networks is incommensurate with any agency/structure dualism. Nor does ANT conceptualize agency as an individuated source of empowerment rooted in conscious intentions that mobilize action. Instead, ANT focuses on the circulating forces that get things done through a network of elements acting upon one another:

> Action is not done under the full control of consciousness; action should rather be felt as a node, a knot, and a conglomerate of many surprising sets of agencies that have to be slowly disentangled. It is this venerable source of uncertainty that we wish to render vivid again in the odd expression of actor-network. (Latour, 2005, p. 44)

What appears to be the teacher's agency is an effect of different forces including actions, desires, capacities and connections that move through her, as well as the forces exerted by the texts and technologies in all educational encounters. While networks and other flows circulate through the teacher's practices, her own actions, desires and so on are not determined by the network, but emerge through the myriad translations that are negotiated among all the movements, talk, materials, emotions and discourses making up the classroom's everyday encounters.

Pondering ANT's utility in overcoming the limitations of intersubjective or humanist conceptions of agency in education, Leander and Lovvorn (2006, p. 301) warn that 'removing the agency of texts and tools in formalizing movements risks romanticizing the practices as well as the humans in them; focusing uniquely on the texts and tools lapses into naïve formalism or technocentrism'. Agency is directly related to the heterogeneity of actors in networked relations. These are not actors plus fields of forces or context, but actants which can only proceed to action by association with others who may surprise or exceed. As McGregor (2004, p. 367) concludes from her study of teachers in science education, 'knowing is a relational effect where pedagogy is a collective accomplishment and learning a situated activity'.

Some immutable mobiles become what Latour (1987) has called obligatory points of passage, central assemblages through which all relations in the network must flow at some time. A teacher's mathematics curriculum guide, for example, functions as an obligatory point of passage. Her lesson plans, her choice of texts and assignments must all at least appear to be aligned with it, and are at least partially translated by its prescriptions. Thus this teacher's knowledge and activity, along with all the other mathematics teachers and classes, those that assist them, the administrators that supervise them and the textbook publishers preparing materials for them, must pass through this obligatory point, this curriculum guide, to form their own networks.

The network effects that produce these immutable mobiles and obligatory points of passage are important dynamics in the power relations circumscribing education. The circulation and effects of these objects can assemble powerful centres that accumulate increasingly wider reaches of networks to hold them in place. Delegation, the ability to act at a distance through objects, is one way that power circulates through a network. How fast these immutable mobiles move, their fidelity or how immutable they really are as they move through diverse networks, and what entities they encounter or damage they sustain to their internal network relations, are questions worthy of exploration in different educational interests.

Scale is another important area for consideration. In fact, as Law and Hetherington (2003) note, if space is performed, if it is an effect of heterogeneous material relations, then distance is also performed. What makes near and far, here or there, is not a static separation between two points that is travelled by some object. Instead, these concepts of distance and location are created by relations that are always changing. When multiple points are linked together through actor-networks, the concepts of micro- and macro- do not hold. The teacher planning her morning class and the final meeting of the curriculum guide developers simply represent different parts of a network that has become extended though space as well as time. There do not exist as separated spaces of the 'local' and 'global', as though these are identifiable and distinct regions. Instead, these are scale effects produced through network relations. A series of intricate links runs among the different enactments of, for example, an educational policy whether visible in OECD documents, school district databases, parent discussions or a teacher's correction of a student. ANT analyses upend and play with notions of scale, eschewing scale as ontologically distinct layers or regions, in ways that help to penetrate some of the more nuanced and multifaceted circulations of power in educational practice and knowledge.

Similarly, macro notions of social structure are not comprehensible in ANT logic. When anyone speaks of a system or structure ANT asks: How has it been compiled? Where is it? Where can I find it? What is holding it together? Soon one sees a number of sites and conduits, and the connections among them. While some have criticized ANT for supposedly failing to address broader macro social structures of capitalism, racism, class–gender relations and so forth in a preoccupation with the local and contingent, ANT commentators reject the dualism of the micro and macro. There are no suprastructural entities, explains Latour (1999, p. 18), because 'big does not mean "really" big or "overall" or "overarching", but connected, blind, local, mediated, related'.

As much as network relations are useful to trace in these dynamics of delegation, obligatory points of passage and scale play, the temptation to collapse all interactions and connections into networks needs to be avoided. While most entities and forces are usefully viewed as effects within an ANT-ish gaze, not all relations that contribute to producing these effects will be networks. There are other types of regions, other kinds of connections, other forms of space and foldings that work alongside and through networks, as Hetherington and Law (2000) describe. Indeed, argues Singleton (2005) in analysing the enactment of public policy, the relative stability of certain networks occurs not through their coherences but through their incoherences and ambivalences. An overly narrow preoccupation with network relations speaks to a bias that will inevitably banish from sight some of the more puzzling messiness of educational phenomena.

This is not to downplay the importance of understanding entities and forces as effects. It is to encourage more open and rich exploration of the multiple forms, lines and textures of materials that come together in different ways to produce these effects. Similarly, learning in ANT logic is not a matter of mental calculation or changes in consciousness. Instead, any changes we might describe as learning, such as new ideas, innovations, changes in behaviour, transformation, emerge through the effects of relational interactions that may be messy and incoherent, and spread across time and space. As Fox (2005) explains in analysing learning processes in higher education, competence or knowledge from an ANT perspective is not a latent attribute of any one element or individual, but a property of some actions rather than others as a network becomes enacted into being. The process of enactment, this interplay of force relations among technology, objects and changes in knowledge at every point in the network, is a continuing struggle. This struggle is learning. This conceptualization offers a way to think about education that steps outside of the 'enculturation' project that typifies pedagogies ranging from the emancipatory to the transmissive. Regardless of ideological persuasion or educative purpose, they claim that education imposes some future ideal on present human subjects and activities with the objective of developing learners' potential to become knowledgeable, civic-minded, self-aware and so forth.

However, since ANT views all things as emerging through their interconnections in networks, where their nature and behaviours are never inherent but are produced through continuous interactions and negotiations, there can be no conception of 'future potential'. This is a powerful counter-narrative to the conventional view of developmentalism that dominates the pedagogical gaze, positioning learners in continual deficit and learning activities as preparation for some imagined ideal. ANT's ontology forces attention on all the work that is too easily swept away by such neat developmental teleologies.

Translation, Devices and Assemblages in Education

In the chapters collected here, authors consider various cases of educational change through the analytic approaches afforded by ANT. Using ANT implies that to theorize is to intervene and experiment rather than to abstract and represent. Thus, the chapters attempt to enact ANT rather than simply, and as we have largely done in this introduction, enact about ANT. As Jan Nespor points out, ANT's focus on objects such as technological 'devices' can unsettle the ways we consider educational change: 'redrawing our understandings of the relations of globalizing and localizing processes, slow and fast networks—and of drawing attention to devices as relatively neglected elements of change processes'. In one case, Nespor follows the many translations enacted in setting up instructional television at one university during the 1970s, and its evolution in subsequent decades to interactive video. The translations link global networks such as the ITV device itself, broadcasts, visions for educational technology, etc. with local networks such as classrooms, curricula and the technology unit in the university. Nespor finds that some of these translations are reversible or short-lived, while others are 'irreversible' and persistent, just as some networks such as technological product development are 'speeded-up' while others such as behaviourist pedagogy are 'slow, congealed'.

He shows that the challenge for those entrusted with managing educational change is to articulate these different networks at play to bring them 'into sync' at appropriate times for different audiences such as professors, administrators, programmers and the State Commission. Nespor contrasts this example with a moving narrative of developing assistive technology for a boy with severe cerebral palsy to enable him to take tests in school. The device emerged through translations such as physical 'tinkering' and experimenting, articulating with and attempting translations of other global networks such as administrative record-keeping and exclusionary practices of segregating special education students. In both cases, he shows how devices translate, how phenomena can be seen and produce major changes in their organizations. Yet the relative 'success' of the devices is ambiguous, and the devices themselves, their contexts of production and the changes they generate differ dramatically.

A fundamental and ubiquitous activity of educational change is the everyday implementation of prescribed curriculum. Drawing upon a case study developed elsewhere (Fenwick & Edwards, 2010), Richard Edwards employs the ANT conceptions of translation and token to examine how this implementation occurs—not as diffusion of the prescription, but as multiple enactments. His case studies, classes for vocational cooking skills in a local UK college and a UK school, reveal the diverse connections among conversations, tastings and objects ranging from students' iPods, white chef coats and textbooks to the cooking knives, pots and smells. Edwards traces the processes through which curriculum-making occurs as a series of network effects through the myriad objects that weave and glue together in classroom activity. As he follows these networks, some embedded in objects or trailed into the class activities from wider outside networks, and others emerging in the everyday entanglement of these entities, he shows how curriculum-making is necessarily multiple and heterogeneous. Enactment of the prescribed, standardized curriculum, therefore, is always a betrayal of the prescription, always a new series of surprising translations.

Over the years, Mary Hamilton has drawn upon ANT to explore how an international marker of educational standards, the International Adult Literacy Survey, both emerged but also how it is translated into policy and practice at different scales. Her chapter focuses in particular on the English Skills for Life policy. She draws upon the early concepts of the moments of translation through which to trace the ways in which the very notion of Skills for Life becomes stabilized as a policy discourse. The ways in which order is enacted in and through policy and in the process becomes taken for granted or naturalized, while also to be found in ideology critique of policy, can only fully be materially traced through ANT.

The enactment of standards in education is the specific focus of the article by Dianne Mulcahy. She explores the ways in which professional standards for teachers are translated into particular forms of teacher work and identity, drawing upon what she refers to as the ontological turn in ANT at the end of the 1990s. Mulcahy is here referring to the moves by people such as Annemarie Mol and John Law to develop framings that focused specifically on the material and semiotic as integral to each other and on a multiple ontologies view. Much contemporary ANTanalysis has moved from the one world/many perspectives view associated with phenomenology to a many worlds perspective (Mol, 2002). Mulcahy shows the diverse enactments of standards as both representations and as performances, sometimes simultaneously in different sites. For her, 'standards are primarily to be seen not in terms of the intrinsic capabilities or potentialities of teaching professionals, or in terms of an extrinsic language of practice, but rather performances of teaching and learning in networks of practice' (emphasis in original). She concludes that these very different performances ought not to be reconciled, but held together in tension.

Tara Fenwick is also interested in how ANT helps to elaborate the tensions and ambivalences in networked spaces and performances. Drawing upon previous explorations of this issue (Fenwick & Edwards, 2010), she contrasts two cases of educational reform, one a province-wide school improvement initiative in Alberta, Canada that becomes enacted through the enrolment of school districts, staff, parents, unions, etc. This long-standing reform process to support school-based action research projects to enhance student achievement has been deemed a 'success' because of levels of participation and the outcomes achieved. Fenwick traces the diverse networks at play in this policy enactment, showing coexisting counter-networks, ambiguous connections and translations that work in different ways at different points. These activities are all assembled together in varying degrees of tension that seem to be necessary to the overall reform. Fenwick therefore makes visible not only the emergence of the policy network and its effects but also the counter-networks and alternative spatialisations through which the reform is undermined, contested, ignored, etc.

As is the case for many educational researchers, Radhika Gorur shifts the focus to the supranational, and is interested in how a particular entity of educational knowledge emerges in ways that can exercise fundamental change. She chooses as her case the OECD's Programme for International Student Assessment (PISA). Contemporary educational analysts (e.g. Grek, 2009) are increasingly concerned about how PISA is being used to govern education transnationally and to translate complex educational processes into static data. Gorur, however, is more interested in how PISA as a form of knowledge with apparent universal acceptance and impact came into being. She follows a method developed by Latour to trace how certain forms of scientific knowledge emerge and become powerful. Such knowledge achieves stabilization through everyday material practices that combine and align wide-ranging objects, ideas and behaviours. In her study of PISA's architects and decision-makers, Gorur adopts this ANT sensibility to examine how PISA knowledge is produced by assembling and connecting a vast array of information from diverse locations and contexts into a single spatio-temporal frame.

PISA as an entity of knowledge is thus shown not only to be relational and continuously performative, but also precarious, held together through ongoing work that sustains its connections and productions—work that can be interrupted, weakened and even refused.

Conclusion

In its insistence on attending to these minute interactions, the precise ways in which they occur as well as their effects, ANT analyses challenge many assumptions under-pinning certain educational conceptions of development and learning, agency, identity, knowledge and teaching, policy and practice. ANT analyses make visible the rich assortments of mundane things at play in educational events and how they are con-nected. The examination of the different processes and moments at work in translation, in particular, extends beyond a simple recognition that artifacts and humans are con-nected in social and cognitive activity. In Latour's (1999, p. 17) summation, ANT's main contribution is to 'transform the social from what was a surface, a territory, a province of reality, into a circulation', where time and space are understood to result from particular interactions of things. ANT's conception of symmetry unlocks a pre-occupation with the human, the intersubjective and the meaning, and refuses a rigid separation between material and immaterial, human and nonhuman objects. In tracing what things do and how they came to be enacted, ANT analyses offer a method for picking apart assumed categories and structures in education, some of which appear to exert power across far-flung distances and temporal periods. For analyzing politics and policy in educational research, Nespor (2002, p. 376) argues that ANT raises important questions about 'how and in what forms people, representations and artifacts move, how they are combined, where they get accumulated, and what happens when they are hooked up with other networks already in motion'. ANT analyses not only can perform the shifting locus of power, how different actors are dominant at different times within different networks, but also show the nuances and ambivalences within this perfor-mance of power. Perhaps, as Neylund (2006, p. 45) puts it, ANT's most important contribution to education is providing an entry point to better understand 'mundane masses (the everyday and the humdrum that are frequently overlooked), assemblages (description of things holding together), materiality (that which does or does not endure), heterogeneity (achieved diversity within an assemblage), and flows/fluidity (movement without necessary stability)'. In attempting to enrol and mobilize ANT into educational research, we would expect parts of that research to become translated into something other than it now mostly is. There is the presumption that this other would also be better, because of, rather than in spite of, the messiness it enacts. Obviously any such translation is incomplete and fragile.

References

Barad, K. (2007) *Meeting the Universe Halfway* (Durham, Duke University Press).

Callon, M. (1986) Some Elements of a Sociology of Translation: Domestication of the scallops and the fishermen of St Brieuc Bay, in: J. Law (ed.), *Power, Action and Belief: A new sociology of knowledge?* (London, Routledge & Kegan Paul), pp. 196–233.

Edwards, R. (2002) Mobilizing Lifelong Learning: Governmentality in educational practices, *Journal of Education Policy*, 17:3, pp. 353–365.

Edwards, R., Biesta, G. & Thorpe, M. (2009) *Rethinking Contexts of Learning and Teaching* (London, Routledge).

Fenwick, T. & Edwards, R. (2010) *Actor-network Theory and Education* (London, Routledge).

Fenwick, T., Edwards, R. & Sawchuk, P. (2011) *Emerging Approaches to Educational Research: Tracing the sociomaterial* (London, Rouledge).

Fox, S. (2005) An Actor-network Critique of Community in Higher Education: Implications for networked learning, *Studies in Higher Education*, 30:1, pp. 95–110.

Frankham, J. (2006) Network Utopias and Alternative Entanglements for Educational Research and Practice, *Journal of Education Policy*, 21:6, pp. 661–677.

Grek, S. (2009) Governing by Numbers: The PISA 'effect' in Europe, *Journal of Education Policy*, 24:1, pp. 23–37.

Hacking, I. (2000) *The Social Construction of What?* (Cambridge, MA, Harvard University Press).

Harmon, G. (2007) The Importance of Bruno Latour for Philosophy, *Cultural Studies Review*, 13:1, pp. 31–49.

Hassard, J., Law, J. & Lee, N. (1999) Introduction: Actor-network theory and managerialism, *Organization*, 6:3, pp. 387–391.

Hetherington, K. & Law, J. (2000) After Networks, *Environment and Planning D: Space and Society*, 18, pp. 127–132.

Latour, B. (1987) *Science in Action: How to follow scientists and engineers through society* (Cambridge, MA, Harvard University Press).

Latour, B. (1999) On Recalling ANT, in: J. Hassard & J. Law (eds), *Actor Network Theory and After* (Oxford, Blackwell Publishers/The Sociological Review).

Latour, B. (2005) *Reassembling the Social: An introduction to actor-network theory* (Oxford, Oxford University Press).

Law, J. (1999) After ANT: Complexity, naming and topology, in: J. Hassard & J. Law (eds), *Actor Network Theory and After* (Oxford, Blackwell Publishers/The Sociological Review), pp. 1–14.

Law, J. & Hetherington, K. (2003) *Materialities, Spatialities, Globalities* (Lancaster, Department of Sociology, Lancaster University). Available at: http://www.comp.lancs.ac.uk/sociology/soc029jl.html

Law, J. & Singleton, S. (2005) Object Lessons, *Organization*, 12:3, pp. 331–355.

Leander, K. M. & Lovvorn, J. F. (2006) Literacy Networks: Following the circulation of texts, bodies, and objects in the schooling and online gaming of one youth, *Cognition & Instruction*, 24:3, 291–340.

McGregor, J. (2004) Spatiality and the Place of the Material in Schools, *Pedagogy, Culture & Society*, 12:3, pp. 347–347.

McLean, C. & Hassard, J. (2004) Symmetrical Absences/Symmetrical Absurdity: Critical notes on the production of actor-network accounts, *Journal of Management Studies*, 41:3, pp. 493–519.

Miettinen, R. (1999) The Riddle of Things: Activity theory and actor-network theory as approaches to studying innovations, *Mind, Culture and Activity*, 6, pp. 170–195.

Mol, A. (2002) *The Body Multiple: Ontology in medical practice* (Durham, NC, Duke University Press).

Mol, A. & Law, J. (1994) Regions, Networks and Fluids: Anaemia and social topology, *Social Studies of Science*, 24, pp. 641–671.

Mulcahy, D. (2007) Managing Spaces: (Re)working relations of strategy and spatiality in vocational education and training, *Studies in Continuing Education*, 29:2, pp. 143–162.

Murdoch, J. (1998) The Spaces of Actor-network Theory, *Geoforum*, 29, pp. 357–374.

Murdoch, J. (2006) *Post-structuralist Geography: A guide to relational space* (London, Sage).

Nespor, J. (1994) *Knowledge in Motion: Space, time and curriculum in undergraduate physics* (London, Routledge).

Nespor, J. (2002) Networks and Contexts of Reform, *Journal of Educational Change*, 3, pp. 365–382.

Neylund, D. (2006) Dismissed Content and Discontent: An analysis of the strategic aspects of actor-network theory, *Science, Technology, Human Values*, 31:1, pp. 29–51.

Singleton, V. (2005) The Promise of Public Health: Vulnerable policy and lazy citizens, *Environment and Planning D: Society and Space*, 23, pp. 771–786.

Strathern, M. (1996) Cutting the Network, *Journal of the Royal Anthropological Institute*, 2, pp. 517–535.

Waltz, S. B. (2006) Nonhumans Unbound: Actor-network theory and the reconsideration of 'things' in educational foundations, *Journal of Educational Foundations*, 20:3/4, pp. 51–68.

1
Devices and Educational Change

JAN NESPOR

> Things are thick with power relations and politics. (Bijker, 2007 p. 115)

This paper examines two cases of device-mediated educational change. One involves a computer-assisted interactive video module that provided a half-hour of instruction for a university course, the other an assistive communication device that proved a supposedly retarded pre-school child to be intelligent. Both were created in the mid-1980s, in sites roughly 30 miles apart.

The interactive video was viewed as a success and won support for its makers; the assistive communication device was rejected and its maker cautioned against repeating such work. Two decades later there are no records or organizational memories of the devices (save those of their makers), but both, I'll argue, were key events in processes of significant organizational transformation.

I have two aims in examining these processes. One is to shed light on the roles of devices in organizational transformations initiated by middle-level workers such as technicians and teachers. I'll argue that device mediated changes, rather than the pre-defined outcomes of planned efforts, or the products of activity systems organized around explicit objectives, are effects of non-linear processes arising out of improvisations that 'continuously generat[e] new results' (Abbott, 2005a, p. 402) across the worker's career. Devices are key to these improvisations: They shape change by slowing things down (orienting work around devices that don't exist yet and require indefinite development processes), or speeding things up (creating devices that seem to do in a short span what otherwise requires long, complex interaction); they re-shape relations among organizations by enrolling allies, or weaken organizational boundaries by making them vulnerable to formerly excluded claimants. Finally, devices can be used to reorganize agency itself in core organizational activities—shifting the location or attribution of who does what, shifting participants from one actor category to another, or creating new categories of agents. Each of these uses appears in the cases described below.

The second aim of the paper is to develop theoretical tools for analyzing such change processes. Although I draw ideas from several fields, the basic perspective taken derives from actor network theory (ANT), 'a disparate family of material-semiotic tools, sensibilities, and methods of analysis that treats everything in the social and natural worlds as a continuously generated effect of the webs of relations within which they are located' (Law, 2009, p. 141). The next section outlines how I want to engage this perspective.

Researching Education Through Actor-Network Theory, First Edition. Edited by Tara Fenwick and Richard Edwards.
Chapters © 2012 The Authors. Book compilation © 2012 Philosophy of Education Society of Australasia.

Devices and Distribution in Actor Network Theory

ANT tells us that we are what we are by virtue of our associations—the ways 'our' identities, thoughts, and actions are produced and spread through people, things, situations, and structures (Law, 1994, pp. 100–101; cf. Lave, 1988; Hutchins, 1995). The idea is not that there are no differences between people and things, but that they are not and cannot be separated. We can move through different settings, use different artifacts and tools, and interact with other people in myriad ways, but we can't get outside such relations. Detachment and de-contextualization can only be accomplished through re-attachment and re-contextualization. As Munro (1996) puts it, you can only go from one network configuration to another—'one is never traveling out from a place (the core self) and then returning ... the only movement is one of circulation: around and around from figure to figure' (pp. 263–264).

As the term 'actor network' implies, people and networks are thus 'co-extensive' (Callon & Law, 1997, p. 169). Even our thoughts are network effects:

> Parts of our selves extend beyond the skin in every imaginable way ... Our memories are in families and libraries as well as inside our skins; our perceptions are extended and fragmented by technologies of every sort ... . When we use the shorthand 'individual' or 'individual cognition', we are thus only pointing to a *density*. (Star, 1995, pp. 19–20; Latour, 2005, p. 211)

Devices are necessarily central to any account in which 'the social' is thus 'materially heterogeneous' (Callon & Law, 1997, p. 167). What this means is that we have to treat interaction as involving not just physically co-present humans but artifacts and environments which congeal past actions—'new hybrid social-and-material practices are constrained and enabled by equally hybrid preexisting practices' (Law & Singleton, 2000, p. 766)—and mediate the ongoing transactions of people widely separated in time and space. From this perspective, agency, the 'capacity to act and to give meaning to action' (Callon, 2005, p. 4), is not a monopoly of bounded human individuals but instead a 'relational effect' (Law, 1994, p. 100; Callon & Law, 1995, p. 502), possible only by virtue of the fact that people 'hook up' (Latour, 1999, p. 18) with institutions, buildings, landscapes, discourses, artifacts, microbes, and the rest, all of which are also networks or 'assemblages' (Cooper, 1998). 'Action, including its reflexive dimension that produces meaning, takes place in hybrid collectives comprising human beings as well as material and technical devices, texts, etc.' (Callon, 2005, p. 4).

The emphasis in ANT is less on the structure of such hybrids than the movement of their constitutive associations across times and spaces. Networks are treated not as stable structures in static landscapes but as contingent effects of 'translations'—the term ANT practitioners give to the 'displacement, drift, invention, mediation, the creation of a link that did not exist before and that to some degree modifies two elements or agents' (Latour, 1994, p. 32). In some cases translations become relatively stabilized and generate organizational structures, infrastructural categories, and well-defined paths for getting things done. But stability can be difficult to achieve and sustain, and often doesn't take a form foreseen by those who accomplish it.

ANT is less a theory of such processes than a set of assumptions and conceptual tools for studying them. Individually these assumptions are not unique to ANT (e.g. Ingold,

2000, pp. 304–5; Lang, 1993; Hutchins, 1995; Fuchs, 2001), but ANT's ways of formulating and combining them have an entailing incompleteness that pushes us towards empirical engagement. As Law (2009) explains, describing ANT in the abstract 'misses the point because it is not abstract but is grounded in empirical case studies. We can only understand the approach if we have a sense of those case studies and how these work in practice' (p. 141).

At the same time, these case studies should have a heavy theoretical recoil. Each involves a translation of ANT itself, pushing the uses of its tools and methods, challenging its sensibilities. The two cases examined here, for example, raise at least the following questions.

First, *how* are associations among people and things accomplished? There are different ways to 'circulate', 'delegate', 'sum', and 'shift down', and Latour (1996b) acknowledges that ANT 'is an extremely bad tool for differentiating associations. It gives a black and white picture not a colored and contrasted one' (p. 380). A speed bump, to take one of his examples, may be 'full of engineers and chancellors and lawmakers, commingling their wills and their story lines with those of gravel, concrete, paint, and standard calculation' (Latour, 1994, p. 41), but the question is how and why 'commingling' happens—for example, how important to a given outcome is the sequencing of assembly, the pacing of composition, the specific mix of the elements associated, whether a given element is essential to the mix or open to substitution, and whether the associations are reversible or easily changed. Do associations and delegations come slowly and incrementally, allowing different kinds of uses at different stages as a device takes form (or as different versions of a device are produced), or do commitments come together all at once (the organization bets on a particular product)? Are commitments large at the outset or do they gradually build? How does one translation relate to a preceding sequence of translations (e.g., Latour, 1996a, p. 91; Law & Callon, 1992, p. 52)?

Second, if body, agency, and mind are distributed networks, how are they made to look like discrete, bounded entities? It may be true that we commonly 'localize agency as singularity—usually singularity in the form of human bodies', through 'attributions which efface the other entities and relations in the *collectif*, or consign these to a supporting and infrastructural role' (Callon & Law, 1995, pp. 502–503). But ANT does not allow us to naturalize such attributions or take them for granted. We know that people do not always individuate agency in this fashion (e.g. Strauss, 2007; Comaroff & Comaroff, 2001), and the persistence of institutions for producing individual subjects (e.g., Foucault, 1979) and promoting public narratives of 'singularity' (Somers & Block, 2005) suggest that such attributions are unstable and require continuous effort. It is as plausible for people to see cognition and agency as distributed or 'stretched out' across people and things as to think it intra-individual.

Third, terms like 'artifact' and 'non-human' (Barron, 2003) are inclusive by design, but as such deflect attention from questions of who makes (or can make) a certain kind of device, who controls use of the device, how access to it is organized, who supplies the power for it, what kinds of products it makes, how it moves, and how it is made visible to different observers (cf. Kirsch & Mitchell, 2004).

Fourth, ANT's analyses of technological change often bracket focal devices (as I do here)—an aircraft, a self-coupling train car—and treat the networks and translations out of which they percolate as being about those devices (I try not to). The obvious point is that such processes are often about other things besides or instead of the focal object. The speed bump may not be what the engineers and chancellors were making, but something that was made because or in spite of other things they did. This may not be relevant to an ANT account of 'speed bumps', but it may be what matters to the people involved. If we take 'identity' to mean 'an actor's experience of a category, tie, role, network, or group, coupled with a public representation of that experience ... not private and individual but public and relational' (Tilly, 2002, p. 75), organizations are not only about 'work', 'activity systems'—or devices—but also about people and groups making identities through articulations with devices.

Finally, the individuals ANT takes as points of entry in tracing networks are usually high-status participants—officials, administrators, 'engineers, technicians, and technocrats'—situated in 'their own separate world' (Latour, 1996a, p. vii). ANT foregrounds activity defined from these standpoints rather than, for example, those of mid-level workers doing things administrators might not care about or approve of. The two cases that follow, by contrast, focus on how middle-level workers in organizations thread connections among devices and different fields of action, and how the devices simultaneously reshape the workers' organizational worlds. I argue that in these processes the organizations themselves change—though not necessarily as the narratives attached to the devices imply. As Ferguson (1990) notes in another context, 'it may be that what is most important about a "development" project is not so much what it fails to do but what it does do; it may be that its real importance in the end lies in the "side effects" ' (p. 254; but contrast Hirschman, 1991, pp. 39–42).

Method

The first case examined below, in which a university-based technologist creates an interactive video teaching device, is based on data drawn from a 1997–2004 study of the introduction of computer-mediated instruction at an American research university (Nespor, 2006). That work involved interviews with administrators and professors (the main sources of data used here), interviews with students, documentary analysis, and classroom observation. The discussion of the preschool teacher's creation of an augmentative communication device is drawn from an extensive ethnographic study of special education practices across time (1989–1991, 2005–2008). In particular I use interview materials (from 1989 and 2005) and documentary materials tracing the work of a teacher, B. The paper also draws on B's own dissertation account of this work, written in 1992.[1]

Foregrounding the work of two people has drawbacks. As Pierson (2004, p. 141) notes, using individuals as entry points for analyzing organizational change favors a focus on 'particular kinds of actors—entrepreneurs, "skilled social actors", and "losers" '. Czarniawska (2009) adds that such research easily falls into the fallacy of '*post hoc, ergo propter hoc:* when an institution has been established, people who were involved in establishing it are seen as decisive for its establishment' (pp. 438–439). This paper may be guilty on both counts, but I would argue that these two protagonists deserve the attention not only as the earliest makers and users in their organizations of the kinds of educational technologies described, but because these early efforts ramified over the decades into major changes in the organizations, and because both had influence well beyond their organizations on the how such devices came to be used by others. Computer-mediated instruction would have come to the university, and assistive communication devices to the public schools, regardless of whether these two particular people had been involved, but without focusing on individuals we have few ways of understanding or even observing change processes structured across biographical and career-length time frames.

Little 'Demos': Technology and Organizational Identity

Teaching in formal educational settings assumes a web of relations linking teachers, students, schools, and content disciplines. Changing teaching involves changing the translations that generate this web. One way to do this is to work on single elements—for example, train better teachers or create better curricular materials. The approach taken in the case below, by contrast, was to use devices to reconfigure the web of relations connecting university teaching to external networks such as professional organizations and technology corporations.

J, the protagonist of this section, played a key role in this effort. He had arrived at the university in 1971, with the job title of 'producer-director', 'to help set up the Instructional Television' (ITV). ITV was undergoing major transitions at the time. It had prospered through the 1950s and 1960s as a way of improving teaching in the public schools (Berkman, 1977), but funding had begun to dry up, and its future role in elementary and secondary education was looking less promising. In early 1970, ITV's major professional organization, the 'Department of Audiovisual Instruction', had broken from its parent organization, the largest national teacher's union, and renamed itself the 'Association for Educational Communications and Technology' (AECT). About the same time it replaced the term 'audio-visual' in its journal titles with 'technology', shifted its focus from compulsory to post-secondary education, and re-wrote its charter to emphasize 'Educational Technology' instead of 'audiovisual communications'. The former was defined as:

> ... a complex, integrated process, involving people, procedures, ideas, devices and organization, for analyzing problems and devising, implementing, evaluating and managing solutions to those problems, involved in all aspects of human learning. (AECT)

This shift in focus faced a substantial hurdle: In universities, professors control curricula and monopolize access to students. In Barley's (1996) terms, people such as producer-directors are confined to subordinate roles as 'technicians'—operators at 'empirical interfaces' (p. 418) of the work process, responsible for translating representations produced by faculty in otherwise transitory forms (for example, lectures) into more stable and standardized products such as video courses. Such work quickly becomes routine: Instead of an 'artisan' involved in 'the design of things', J became an 'operative' to whom 'their construction' was delegated—a provider of standardized solutions to a finite set of puzzles (Ingold, 2000, pp. 295–296; also Braverman, 1974). Looking back from the late 1990s J recalled working with 'hundreds of faculty' and producing 'close to a thousand [television] programs' over a dozen years. But:

Everything had gotten too formulaic. They came in the door with a problem and I knew 'that's solution 32'—and I'd go make that guy a program. And I knew just about every answer I could think of. So I wanted to do something different.

To do something different he went back to graduate school for a doctorate in Instructional Systems Design. This allowed him to explore innovative uses of instructional technology at other universities:

... there was very early experimentation ... People were trying to uncover how to get away from the linearity of television, to introduce interactive control ... I was intrigued with computer assisted instruction (CAI) as a domain ... .

As phrases like 'experimentation' and 'getting away' imply, there was no orthodoxy or standard model of CAI at the time. Neither, J recalled, was there much awareness or interest in it among administrators at his university: 'nothing like that here, nor any funds to buy anything like that'.

To 'do something different', then, he needed to connect his work at the university to innovative efforts elsewhere, forge a coherent organizational identity from those connections, change his relations with faculty members from operative to artisan, and build an institutional base.

The effort took years, and a key episode shaping the path it followed was the production of a device. After obtaining his doctorate, J had moved to an 'instructional developer' position, and began what he recalled as his 'first significant project' in 1983. It was a collaboration with a professor, S, to make a device that would present content (in video form) and link it with student performance (through a computer program). S recalled that J:

... sent out a memo around campus ... 'If anybody wants to do interactive video, we've got the resources to make it happen' ... . I'd been reading non-stop in trade publications ... sort of computer nerd stuff, you know ... So ... I'd probably read about interactive video ... . And I thought, 'well, what the heck?'

This recruitment strategy made it likely that volunteers would be 'gadget-scientists' (Nutch, 1996)—professors accustomed to dealing with technical issues 'impinging on their work without relying on outside or standardized resources' (p. 215). With such collaborators, and a focus on CAI, the object of work shifted from video production to software coding, a move allowing J to reconfigure work relations: much of the responsibility for writing code fell to S, who recalled spending '500 hours of time [writing code] to produce half an hour of instruction'. The idea, he explained:

... was to videotape some instructional stuff, and create to run parallel to that a program that ran on the Apple IIE ... . And at various points throughout that instruction it would stop and ask a question. For example, if the student got the question right, they would proceed forward according to the software code that I created, and if they got it wrong it would perhaps route them back to some remedial instruction.

Five hundred hours would seem a steep price for 30 minutes of instruction, but instruction wasn't really the focus. Far from transforming teaching and learning, the interactive video project pushed them, and the course itself, out of the frame and centered attention on an idea of 'courseware' embodied by the device. Courseware implies shifts in the location of teaching agency from the instructor to the device, and of design agency from the professor to the instructional technologist—both shifts accomplished through a particular kind of performance, the demonstration. As J explained, such performances constituted the main use of the device:

> We actually used this maybe three or four semesters. Got a whole lot of conference presentations, a couple of articles. Our whole thrust was, 'here's how faculty can get involved in this new kind of way to teach, give students some control over how they learn'.

As S recalled, they traveled around the country:

> ... hauling an APPLE IIE and an APPLE IIE monitor, and a VCR and a big, hopefully a big TV ... and then hooking that all up, and literally demo-ing the ... courseware ... and explaining the how and why and answering questions after it.

Shapin and Schaffer (1985, p. 60) described 17th century scientific illustrations as instruments of 'virtual witnessing'—representations that allowed (or persuaded) dispersed audiences to accept the results of experiments that had been staged in settings distant in time and space. Demonstrations like those of the interactive video, by extension, might be labeled mechanisms for 'witnessing the virtual': They enable audiences to imagine devices that do not exist, by showing them what are said to be precursor artifacts in the hands of people who can supposedly make the real things at a later time. As Barry (1999) notes, 'the idea of the *demo* implies provisionality. A demo model is a display of the possibility of a real object, rather than its actualization. It is a way of showing what can or might be done' (p. 77).

Perhaps as importantly, demonstrations are 'performative' enactments (Law & Singleton, 2000) of possible identity positions for the technology's makers and users. In this case, at least, the demo was a translation device for shifting instructional technologists from operator to artisan positions in the 'standardized package' of methods, technologies, and shared objects through which they and university faculty jointly collaborated to 'construct and solve "doable" problems' (Fujimura, 1992, pp. 176–177). More than this, however, the demo was a device for shifting J's public identity nationally and locally. Recall that an 'identity' consists of a configuration of ties—a particular way of assembling an actor network—coupled to a public narrative. As both an 'autographic' object—'with traceable origins that can be directed attributed to an individual' (J & S), and an 'allographic' object, 'whose origins cannot be traced' (an exemplar of an imagined class of computer-mediated teaching devices) (Bechky, 2003, pp. 741–742; citing Goodman, 1978), the demo was a means of generating a narrative of J and his unit as the local group capable of producing computer mediated teaching (cf. Bechky, 2003, p. 725) *and* as the link connecting the university to a national network of instructional innovation. Indeed, it was one of the mechanisms for creating that national network. If the interactive video as autographic stayed tethered to J's unit, as allographic it could be combined with other demos into collections, then circulated nationally. J recalled that he:

> ... hooked up with several other people doing similar projects. In a span of three years collected, really people all over the country by then who were doing similar projects. And I collected demonstrations of what they were doing and produced several ... anthologies [of] ... people's work at other universities, for AECT, and they sold these tapes.

Collecting conference demos was one way of assembling allies from around the country into something that began to look like a national movement for computer-mediated instruction. This national presence, in turn, made it easier to get federal grants for new demonstration projects with faculty members, and part of this funding could be used to:

> ... buy a lot of equipment. We built up our internal development base in this department. We used it to hire and train a number of people ... We stepped up from really being kind of backwater and really peripheral, really marginal, to having a resource base at least that some people could use. We went through at least three federal grants in different areas to get to that point.

This accumulation of equipment and personnel would have helped to stabilize an identity for 'instructional technology' (IT) on campus, but making it part of the university's core infrastructure meant translating it into a priority of the entity to which the university was answerable: The state. This required another kind of 'inscription device', specifically a 'Task Force'.

By late 1989 the state in which this university was located, like other states, was dealing with the beginnings of an economic recession. Legislators looking for places to cut budgets found higher education a ripe target (Slaughter, 1993), and part of the university's defense was to construct a narrative of itself as an innovator in the development of more efficient means of instruction that would save money later. Information technologies were key to this narrative—again, as they were at universities across the country—and in the university set up a 'Task Force' on 'The Impact of Digital Technologies on the Classroom Environment' to produce a report that would document its commitment. Although professors made up most of the membership, J was the group's staff person—a role in which he 'gave a number of demonstrations'.

The task force translated these demos into a text—a report which claimed that such technologies could radically transform teaching and learning in the university—that moved differently than the demos themselves. In particular, such texts can be understood as programs or scripts offered to more stable and powerful networks, which are encouraged to quote or hybridize them into new texts that can then circulate through different institutional networks and undergo further translations into budget, policy, and legislative documents.

In this case the uptake was quick. By the time the university task force released its report, the State Department of Higher Education had assembled a 'Governor's Commission' to examine state university policy and suggest directions for its development. For its discussion on the role of technology in higher education, the Commission simply appropriated the report of J's task force as a template, quoting liberally from it and closely following its argument. Thus re-situated, the language of the task force report was used to justify state higher education funding decisions as late as 1995. We can label this a 'blowback translation', in which the products of a local actor network travel through a translation circuit and return as the actions of another (more global) network, in which form they reshape the premises of local practice. In this case the blowback benefited J's work unit. New Requests for Proposals for education development projects, for example, funneled money to technology demonstrations of the kind already being pursued by J's and his colleagues. Money from these grants then allowed J to enroll more faculty members in his efforts (giving them summer salary money or buying them out of teaching responsibilities), and to hire:

> ... programmers, an artist, it was a CAI [Computer-Assisted Instruction] development lab that was essentially put together ... . Those projects, plus the earlier work with the federal projects, produced some local content that we could trot out on stage to visitors ... the board ... people in the Provost's office, or to Deans. I remember making a lot of demonstrations, little demos.

J's unit also used money from the state grant to organize a dissemination conference for other State-funded IT projects, and J arranged for AECT to hold its summer technology conference at the same place and time:

> So we used state money and invited faculty from all over the state to come free to this thing, and we also pulled in like 100 people from all around the country for three or four days ... . That was a very significant conference.

In the context of budgetary pressures, the collective performances of these national and local projects would have been significant in part because they demonstrated the extent to which computer-mediated instruction had been translated from a risky inno-vation into a basic institutional commitment, and in part because the presentations would have helped engender a kind of 'professional vision' (Goodwin, 1994): a way of framing and 'coding' teaching so that the audience of administrators and interested faculty would see it from the particular professional perspective of the instructional technologist—as something doable by machine. Such a framing allowed legislators to draw the inference that it might be possible, in the words of one university administrator, to 'capitalize the cost of education'. J and the other technology advocates at the university did not explicitly endorse this idea, but neither did they resist it:

> There are people [at the state level, in the legislature] saying you use technol-ogy to save money. We do not answer that directly. We just keep going. Because we were quite certain that you would not save money.

This is not a case of allowing others to delude themselves to your advantage, but more like an offering in a speculative market on instructional derivatives: the translation of some immediate, situated activity in itself not yet or not obviously productive (devices like the interactive video), into a contingent future (a university offering computer-mediated courses), that might in turn be translated into legislative policy (a less expen-sive university system). One result at the local level was the internal reallocation of university monies to increase support for Educational Technologies. As J recalled, the support flowed:

... into us, into this group. And why this group? This group was *the* group that had a long-standing working relationship with faculty on instruction. Not *many* faculty, but we were well perceived as the people, if you had an issue with technology or media or teaching, we were the group you would talk to.

ANT researchers might say that at this point the unit became a kind of 'obligatory passage point' in the university's efforts to promote instructional technology. For Law and Callon (1992), this would be a key point of stabilization. They argue that the success of a 'technological project' depends on whether it can 1) construct 'a global network that will for a time provide resources of various kinds in the expectation of an ultimate return'; 2) construct a 'local network using the resources provided by the global network to ultimately offer a material, economic, cultural, or symbolic return to actors lodged in the global network'; and 3) 'impose itself as an obligatory point of passage between the two networks' (1992, p. 46). In other words, to stabilize themselves, actor networks draw on relatively more stabilized (which usually means more extensive or 'global') circuits for materials, money, or discursive resources. In this instance there were a number of these networks—the computer industry, the AECT, the university system, state legislators, and so on—and multiple 'local' networks as well, including J's technology unit, the university faculty, the administrators, which were in turn already tightly linked to global networks (design fields, academic disciplines, the state university system). A lot of the action thus involves re-articulating local associations among the global networks—redrawing the boundaries of the university, or at least the boundaries of university teaching, to bring it under the partial purview of external networks like those of instructional designers (as much part of the corporate and military sphere as the university)—in ways that don't so much make a particular configuration of associations 'obligatory' as make it predictable and easy to use.

That is, unlike true 'obligatory passage points'—translations that become increasingly costly to reverse over time as more is made to depend on them and other options disappear (Callon, 1991, pp. 149–150; also Pierson, 2004, pp. 20–21)—some identity networks expand and stabilize by organizing themselves through devices and projects easily made and abandoned (cf. Singleton & Michael, 1993). J did not become lastingly identified with a specific device (the instructional video dissipated as soon as its dem-onstration value dried up). Keeping associations discretionary and reversible, keeping the exact nature of the devices and the extent of their use ambiguous, means that the translation of work and device into financial costs and returns can be largely controlled by developers and backers. It also allows the development process to unfold incremen-tally, and thus blunts potential resistance from administrators and faculty by allowing them to retain substantial control over timing decisions regarding use and resource commitment. We might call all this a form of 'identity infrastructuring' in which the products of change are not just or even primarily specific devices, or the conduct of a target activity (e.g. teaching), but the relations that create and stabilize institutional actors or identities.

But what if there are no global networks—or only antagonistic ones? What if ties can't be discretionary or loose? What if shifting organizational borders brings in new actors who want control of key organizational decisions? What if a device doesn't change or improve (or promise to change and improve) existing local practices but changes categories in ways that create problems for other people and entail significant costs? These are some of the questions raised by the second case, but to get to them we have to start with a more fundamental question.

Devices and Change: Tinkering, Cartesian Fixes, Brokerage

How do we know that children who have never spoken, signed, pointed, or controlled their movements enough to use standard communicative devices are capable of the kinds of thoughts, feelings, desires, and rationality we attribute to ourselves? Most Western philosophical perspectives simply assume communicative bodies (e.g. Berg & Akrich, 2004; Merleau-Ponty, 1963; Gallagher, 2005; Grosz, 1994; Shilling, 2005; cf. Moser, 2003). It's understood that people can lose access to embodied abilities they formerly possessed, or be born without certain abilities as normally constituted, but we usually assume they have access to at least some familiar communicative channels, or had access in the past, and thus we read their situations as component breakdowns in intelligent bodies and assume it's possible to communicate with them, or restore communicativeness with appropriate prostheses. To take a famous example, we can trace the physicist Stephen Hawking's biographical trajectory back through amyotrophic lateral sclerosis to a previous embodiment in which he used a full range of communicative channels: thus we assume he remains intelligent and that he can communicate if we provide the right assistance (Stone, 1995; Mialet, 2003).

But how we would know 'Stephen Hawking' were intelligent if he had been born with his late-in-life physical capabilities? He wouldn't be the same 'Stephen Hawking'—his actual present depends on his abled past—but how would we have known that we could communicate with such an embodied person? More generally, how do people *born* with limited or no use of their hands, who cannot move their bodies through the world at will or without the use of 'instruments', become recognizable as intelligent and potentially communicative? How are they made so? It is one thing to say we are all networks, that cognition and communication are intrinsically distributed, but how do we *re-make* such networks for people currently assembled in subordinating or oppressive relations—especially when there are not maps or assembly diagrams available? How do we even convince others that such networks are possible? These were hard questions in the mid-1980s, and B, the person we follow through this section, had to answer them under time pressures from the inside of a preschool classroom.

B had begun teaching at 40, with an English degree and Montessori certification—the latter qualifying her to teach special education in the eyes of the school district. The preschool class she was assigned contained a mix of children, from 'mildly LD [Learning Disabled], a little bit speech impaired, blind and brilliant ... [to] severely mentally and motor impaired'. When the children turned six years old they received official special education labels. Those deemed 'mildly' disabled, a little impaired, or brilliant were sent to regular schools. Those said to have significant cognitive disabilities were sent to a segregated school for the 'severely and profoundly' and 'trainable mentally handicapped'. Children who didn't speak or sign were placed in one of these latter categories. 'One of the ways they could get these people put in the severely profoundly handicapped classes', B explained, 'is they could say they were untestable' (1989 interview).

School officials considered Michael, the child at the center of the story in this section, one of these 'untestable' students. Diagnosed with 'severe mixed spastic athetoid cerebral palsy', he sometimes moved his head to indicate yes and no, but could not stand, speak, hold objects, or point (B, 1992, p. 224). Officials defined him as severely cognitively impaired. His mother concurred. B, however, came to hold a different view, in part from experiences like the one recounted below.

Following rain one day, B had taken her preschool class outside to the playground, where everyone removed their shoes and splashed in puddles like the characters in the book she was reading to the class, Beatrix Potter's *Jemima Puddle Duck*. The translated embodiments of this event—the children becoming ducklings, turning the book's words and pictures into corporeal experience—also entailed transformations in Michael's bodily incorporation into the class:

> I unstrapped Michael from his chair and held him upright against me as we jumped and splashed. I had seldom heard him laugh so heartily or look so enthusiastic about being a part of things. Because I was holding him upright the way he might be if he could stand, children were holding his hand and relating with eye-to-eye contact at a level he was not used to. (B, 1992, pp. 226–227)

When the rains resumed and B took the children inside for a nap, 'Michael started howling ... He kept looking at the tumbling mat and back to me and making noises louder than I'd ever heard him make' (B, 1992, p. 227). B could have treated these howls as indications of physical discomfort, but instead she took them as what Goffman (1978) called 'response cries':

> Unable to shape the world the way we want to, we displace our manipulation of it to the verbal channel, displaying evidence of our alignment to the on-going events; the display takes the condensed, truncated form of a discretely-articulated non-lexicalized expression. (p. 801)

Reading the howls as protests at the story's interruption, B asked, ' "Do you still want to be Puddle Duck and go to bed?" He nodded and howled in a different way. So I continued as if we were still part of the story' (B, 1992, pp. 226–227). Concluding the book's narrative through this collective performance shifted Michael's status from that of seemingly passive participant to active agent—someone who did the same things as the other kids, and whose expression of will had to be acknowledged by the teacher.

It is impossible, of course, to reconstruct exactly *how* such events convinced B of Michael's intelligence, but the transformation of the physical and narrative organization of the classroom would be part of the answer. Holding Michael changed his bodily orienta- tion to his classmates and allowed B to feel his embodied participation and track his eye gaze in new ways. Making puddles and towels available gave him a non-lexicalized way to participate in the event—participation he extended first through laughter, then 'howls' as the rain initiated a cascade of binaries—outside/inside; story/no-story, laughter/crying, yes/no—which he could mesh with the ability to move his head and vocalize (cf. Ferm, Ahlsen, & Bjorck-Akesson, 2005, pp. 19–20; Mialet, 2003, pp. 588–589).

Such engagements would have been legible as 'intelligence', however, only because B's extended observations and interactions with Michael and students like him—her experiences of 'managing bodies across private and social spaces' (Kelly, 2005, pp. 190–191; Goldbart & Marshall, 2004, p. 202)—had engendered what Csordas (1993) calls 'somatic modes of attention': 'culturally elaborated ways of attending to and with one's body in surroundings that include the embodied presence of others' (p. 138). As she soon discovered, insights grounded in such relations were not easily reproduced for school officials whose interactions with children like Michael were comparatively brief and superficial, and whose logics of assessment derived from fields like psychology, where as late as the mid-1990s researchers insisted on the 'strong presumptive relationship, in general, between overt production and actual ability' (Jacobson, Mulick & Schwartz, 1995, p. 757).

'Overt production' in this logic did not refer to performances like Michael's in the *Jemima Puddle Duck* story but to 'production' within the spatial and temporal frames of testing events. As Foucault (1979) suggests, a test 'introduces individuality into the field of documentation' (p. 189) and constructs an individual in ways that allow him to be 'be described, judged, measured, compared with others, in his very individuality' (p. 191). In ANT terms tests hide our network-qualities—our histories, resources, tools, and allies—and inscribe us as discrete packages of abilities and potentials defined in terms of measurable categorical essences (e.g. 'intelligence'). One of the perverse entailments of the logic is that the right to be tested becomes a core element of the right to have rights—to be a citizen. To say that Michael was 'untestable' meant that he could not be separated from his associations, and thus lacked measurable essences and 'actual ability'. For administrators this meant he belonged in the segregated school for children with severe disabilities. Nothing B said could change their minds:

> One administrator had patted me on the back and assured me, these children were born limited. 'It's just sad, but it doesn't do to get over-involved'. Another administrator, in a less sympathetic manner, admonished me that I was just going to feed the parents' unrealistic view of what these students were capable of. (B, 1992, pp. 235–6).

To keep Michael out of this school and 'prove his intelligence' (p. 234), then, B decided to figure out a way to test him.

Unlike J, who could redefine teaching as that which his device did (making actual teachers and students unnecessary for the demonstrations), B's problem was to make a device that would be invisible, something administrators could treat, like Stephen Hawking's devices (Mialet, 2003), a 'pliant and diligent slave' (Latour, 1994, p. 31), as a passive prosthetic that 'transports meaning ... without transformation' (Latour, 2005, p. 39). If a 'Cartesian view of the world' is defined as the idea that 'human subjects or cognitive systems' are 'completely different from objects, i.e., material givens or artefacts' (Lang, 1993, p. 88), what B was after was a Cartesian Fix, a way to make Michael's mind visible as separate and distinct not only from his body, but from her efforts and any testing device.

Finding such a device wasn't easy. J was aware of global networks and could study exemplars elsewhere before he initiated the interactive video project. B, too, saw computers as the part of the answer, but beyond that had no clear idea of what to look for:

> This was just on my own ... I called all the universities around and I said, 'I'd like to take a course on how to use computers with people who are really disabled'. Nobody had a course ... . But because I'd called, a secretary remembered me when somebody got sick and dropped out of one of their research projects. And she called me and invited me to join this well-funded thing that gave me thousands of dollars of equipment. I had never turned a computer on. They didn't know that. So I just hung low and kept my mouth shut 'til I figured it out. And that was how I got my training initially. (2005 Interview)

Learning as she went, B first gave Michael an off-the-shelf scanning board that should have allowed him to indicate words and pictures by using switches to turn on lights. His hands flailed, however, and he quickly became exhausted. Moreover, the lights were so small that 'at times Michael didn't seem to know where he had stopped the light or which answer he had chosen' (B, 1992, pp. 236–237).

School administrators could have read these difficulties as failures of 'overt production' and taken them as evidence of Michael's untestable, retarded condition. The problem for them was political as well as empirical. Scientists working in new areas, for example,

> ... often have an agonizing choice to make: at what point have they done enough? ... A negative result or a set of such results may demonstrate, not the non-existence of some disputed phenomenon, but a failure of experimental technique. (Pinch, Collins & Carbone, 1996, pp. 169–170)

The school administrators, by contrast, also would have had to consider how much time and money should be expended to see if Michael, however configured, could hit the right switches. As they'd already categorized him as constitutively unable to perform intelligently, B's efforts would have appeared not just foolish but unethical and wasteful, taking resources from other children. For B, by contrast, this was not an experimental discovery problem and Michael's intelligence not a 'disputed phenomenon': She'd witnessed it already in events like the *Puddle Duck* episode. For her the problem was to close the gap (Lave, 1988) between what she'd seen manifested over time in embodied engagements, and what could be seen in brief and publicly reproducible demonstrations.

There's a parallel in Disability Studies, where theorists and activists distinguish between 'impairment' (limitations on activity produced by physical or intellectual conditions) and 'disability' (limitations produced by the social organization of activities). Being blind as opposed to sighted, for example, entails differences in access to certain phenomena, but the disabling implications of these differences for, say, one's success in school with sighted peers, are socially produced. In these terms B's problem was to shift understanding of Michael's overt production from the category of impairment to that of disability.

Impairment is far from stable, however (Thomas, 2004, p. 574). As Erevelles (2002, p. 16) argues, bodies are not static 'pre-social' (or asocial) bundles of capacities (normal or impaired, cf. Kelly, 2005). What 'bodies' (and minds) are capable of depends on the networks of constant translation out of which they're assembled—their diets, environments, physical therapy, prosthetics, interactional opportunities and so forth. To get Michael tested, then, B had to assemble an entire network.

She had little idea how to go about this. Few people in the region could help (the university that gave her the computer was 120 miles away), and the low profile of the assistive technology field in the mid-1980s (Zangari, Lloyd & Vicker, 1994, p. 49) left her without access to works of potential relevance (e.g. Goossens, 1989). She had no training in technology, either, although she had watched her father, a repairman, at work. Her first idea was to get a circuit diagram for a scanning board from the state department of education and build one with bigger lights for Michael. She did, but the board didn't work. A teacher at the local vocational-technical school explained that the diagram was incorrectly drawn. When volunteers at the school built a working version, however, it turned out Michael lacked the muscle control to use the switches. B tried anchoring his arm to limit the involuntarily movements, but this quickly tired him, so she changed the type of switch to make it more compatible with the arm movements Michael could comfortably make. Now the problem was that the movements were so forceful he broke the switches. To deal with this, B taught herself soldering and began experimenting with different switch materials and placements (B, 1992, p. 240).

> I didn't even know the difference between rosin core and the other kind of solder. And I had to go and buy things and then adapt them by using this rosin core solder ... . I had to go and figure this out. (2005 interview)

The university project mentioned earlier gave her access to help she couldn't get locally:

> They put us on an internet connection when there was no web ... . And one night I actually got on ... sort of live at the time. A guy in Seattle talked me through how to solder this thing. And I was very nervous 'cause I'd paid $80 for this equipment. If I had broken it no one would reimburse me. They [the school administrators] didn't even know what I was trying to do. (2005 interview)

She had to hide her work from administrators in part because she was 'tinkering' with the device, that is, making it through 'a progressive selection of what works' in a particular situation (Knorr-Cetina, 1979, p. 369), 'using what is at hand, making-do, using things for new purposes, patching things together, and so on' (Clark & Fujimura, 1992, p. 11). Tinkering itself is not an illegitimate mode of work, but device-making and intelligence testing were clearly not part of B's job description, and the failures, mistakes, and recursive adjustments inherit in tinkering would likely have been taken as evidence of her incompetence and insubordination—she was, after all, trying to undermine her employer's decision—as well as of Michael's cognitive limits. Unlike J, she worked in an antagonistic environment dominated by a 'greedy' (Coser, 1974) network—a network that monopolizes the institutional or public definition of people by stabilizing associations that position it as gatekeeper or 'obligatory passage point' to resources they depend upon. Indeed, B herself was one of these essential resources, and she had to make the device work right the first time in public or risk a prohibition on further development efforts.

This turned out to involve more than she had anticipated. It became clear that Michael's ability to use the board was located not just in his hands and arms but in the positioning of his hips in the wheelchair and in the wheelchair itself (he was growing and needed a new one). Moreover, the ability to use a scanning board, like all abilities, is relational. Although Michael initially tired quickly, physical therapy helped him build muscle control, and B was able to get the school psychologist to adjust the testing procedures and allow Michael time to move the switches and rest when exhausted. In principle, as Winance (2006, p. 68) notes, this 'process of adjustment is continuous'. In this instance, however, once adjustments had produced a network that allowed Michael to reliably manipulate the switches, the cloistering of the development process could be abandoned, administrators and others informed of the work, and Michael could take the test to demonstrate himself as an intelligent, individuated child.

He did. And the administrators were not happy. 'The Special Ed[ucation] director for the country went to my principal and said, "Tell her not to do that again ... He said, "That's going to lead parents to unrealistic expectations".' B recalled in a 1989 interview:

> You spend your time and efforts and you prove this stuff. You put your own money into the technology because there is no budget for you, and you finally got this thing out, and everybody is going 'Drop dead. Get out of here. This messes up our view of things' ... . I didn't have tenure, and if I'd been younger with a principal who didn't back me up, I would have been out of the school system, really and truly.

She wasn't dismissed, but administrators followed through with their original plans and placed Michael in the segregated school.

The administrators had a reason to be worried. Michael became known locally among parents of children with disabilities as an example of the child-wrongly-presumed-retarded-and-redeemed-through-technology, and they eventually forced the school district to create a special class for him and others in a regular elementary school setting. As B recalled:

> It wasn't six months later they were bringing in the school board and praising me in the papers. You're praised for the wrong thing, and you're damned for the wrong thing. What you really do doesn't get noticed. (2005 interview).

Part of B's inability to control the public narrative of her work—to stabilize a new identity for herself—stemmed from the fact that, unlike J, who finished his doctorate before shifting the focus of his work, the urgency of Michael's situation had forced her to proceed without academic credentials or official license. *After* her work with Michael, however, B did return to graduate school, wrote a dissertation on her work with Michael, and gained a doctorate in Special Education Administration (from the same department in which J earned his, albeit in a different program). By this time, more and more parents were demanding access to alternative testing and assistive technologies for their children. The doctorate, on top of the belated publicity from her work with Michael, allowed B to move from teaching to become a technology consultant and assistive technology trainer.

> I did a lot of training of teachers all over the state ... . Always the school systems were way behind in the technology, and in many cases the parents and

the advocates knew more of what was available. And if they didn't shout and scream and bring an expert, people would not do these things. So the Department of Ed and the various people said 'we've got to train teachers so they know more what to do'. And that was my job. I would run around training teachers. And I would do workshops on a specific device with clips of how my students use it … . After I covered the whole state then I went back [laughs] … I worked in fifty schools … with students from eight school districts.

Some 20 years after her work with Michael, B returned to her old school district as a one-person AT unit (the administrators who had opposed her were long gone). When she'd last been a teacher there,

… the kids who got the AT generally had either people like me who chose them as guinea pigs to help them, or parents who were very vocal and insisting … . They tended to be, in most cases, the better educated parents … . That's not true anymore.

Now there were regulations requiring that AT uses be explored for children with disabilities, global networks developing such technologies, and advocacy groups disseminating information about them to parents. This reshaping of organizational boundaries to open arenas of school practice to the influence of parents and technologists now created problems for B in her role as a technician for the District:

Parents [were] the big movers of assistive technology, initially … . But it turned into being a bit of a problem later because then they would go off to some conference where someone would talk about a particular device and they would come back and demand that device. Well, the problem is if your insurance or your school paid what was then about $3,000 or $4,000 for some big hot-shot device they weren't going to buy another one six-months later when you found out that was the wrong one, and sometimes it really was the wrong one. And I would come in with something that was either more complicated or less complicated and the parents would have a fit because 'so and so said', you know.

Instead of tinkering and demonstrating, B's work now consisted of setting up and programming off-the-shelf devices. In the early days she had known 'every single augmentative communication device on the market [and] … all of the major good software … There wasn't a whole lot'. By 2005 each week seemed to bring a new product with a 100-page manual to master. Although her work now helped scores of children, not just a handful, B was no long an artisan working under the radar but something closer to an operative, an 'accessory to processes whose specification has been laid down in advance' (Ingold, 2000, pp. 295–96). She recalled that her father had:

… loved to take his tool kits everywhere he went. And when I first got into assistive technology, you had to do that. We had to up-end the [wheel] chairs and use our tools ourselves. We can't do that now. We would void warranties … . At first, you felt like you were a repairman, an advocate, a teacher, a designer, but also a lawyer in the middle … . Literally, one-fourth of my house was equipment. I had turned my entire basement into nothing but a work area with a table five times this big with cabinets all around. The reason I did that [was] because no school system would give me the space I needed …

Man, those days are a bit gone by. I now have a closet—unheated, cold, and it gets moved every two years … . But the thing is I do have a lot of money in equipment and devices.

For all these resources, however, she worried about how the devices were being integrated into the children's lives. The extended, inter-corporeal relations through which she had recognized Michael's skills and tinkered him into a successful communicative configuration were impossible to reproduce in the current school context. The technology and her role as technology specialist had shifted the focus to identifying, procuring, programming, and maintaining devices:

The biggest support comes in knowing how the kid learns and how to set it up to get them going and to make them even care about using it. That's harder today …

When I taught I learned why [the children] dropped it. And I adapted it. And then if I noticed they'd give it a little more time, I'd adapt it a little more. Then if I noticed they really did something, then I would figure out what it was that had engaged them. And that's how I would keep it going. Whereas if a person is overwhelmed … . Almost everything that administrators, secretaries, and support people did in those early days is now done by one teacher … I would not go into Special Ed today unless you paid me a million dollars, and … I'd use half of it to pay for assistance.

Conclusions

These last comments remind us that the historical-geographic junctions at which events unfold are keys to their meanings and implications. J and S were working on the problems described here at a time when broad waves of change—computerization, new disability laws—were sweeping through schools, and it might seem that rather than initiating device-mediated change they were surfing the waves of change. But broader movements are made out of the activities of people like J and S. From an ANT perspective, understanding change isn't a matter of locating individuals in 'larger' processes, but of mapping the translations, circuits, and performances that are assembled into such processes. The maps themselves presumably will be unique—historically and geographically specific—but the mechanisms of translation and performance and the strategies of stabilization and change should have relevance beyond the particular case. Just as ANT is empirically entailing—its full meanings emerging through case analyses—so its analyses gain resonance when translated or linked to other studies. I've tried to illustrate this in a limited way by noting some contrasts and similarities across the two cases. Without trying to summarize the work, I'll end by pointing to a few more.

It matters whether people and devices are attached through discretionary or obliga-tory associations. J and S could abandon the interactive video without losing the ability to teach, but Michael would lose a great deal without an assistive communication device (and for a while he did—at first his wheelchair and board were too large to fit in the trailer he shared with his mother and her boyfriend, and he lost access to communicative channels every day when he went home). Along another dimension, however, it was critical to the shift in identity that J was constructing that he remained (at least in the early years, until the task force report and the stabilization of his organizational unit) associated with *some* demonstrable device (hence the chain of grant-funded projects): His identity took years to stabilize. By contrast, Michael's transformation after the public demonstration was irreversible in the same sense that Stephen Hawking's history of communicativeness is irreversible: Denying Michael an assistive communication device does not return him to the category of a 'severely and profoundly handicapped' person. Once it is shown that such devices allow him to perform intelligently, denying him one becomes a category violation and a violation of his rights. Some translations are narratively indelible, then, others performatively contingent.

Associations also need to be differentiated in terms of the delay or immediacy of the translations they effect. As a demonstration of a future device, administrators and professors could invest in J's device or use it without changing what they did in the short term. Since 'courseware' was an unfinished and malleable 'boundary negotiating artifact' (Lee, 2007), it was possible to push decisions about translations indefinitely into the future. B's device, by contrast, allowed Michael to take the test and immediately claim his new identity. As school administrators realized, it also opened the system to immediate demands by other families of supposedly 'untestable' children.

Such differences had implications for the ways organizational boundaries were defined. Instructional technology devices were instruments for shifting the relations of the university to state bureaucracies and professional associations like the AECT. State funding priorities and policy languages became influences on classroom pedagogy in ways they had not been in the past; professors trying to introduce instructional tech-nologies with the help of J's unit found their teaching realigned with instructional design fields.

In B's case, the problem for the school was that Michael's performance was a 'demo' not just of what *he* could do, but of what other children defined as retarded might be able to do with appropriate prostheses. The device did not simply suggest a role for tech-nologists in 'testing', it implied a re-drawing (or weakening) of school boundaries in a way that gave parents grounds for making legal demands for assistive technology.

Finally, although it's been understood since the 19th century that a machine extends in space and motion to include the objects it works upon and the sources of its energy (Ingold, 2000), the cases here ask us to reconsider where artifacts begin and end in time—the temporalities of associations and translations. To make sense of the interactive video or the scanning board we needed to look at the histories of the people who made them, the labs, offices, and work tables they had access to, and the pace of their work against the calendars and time-reckoning systems of their organizations. Things, as ANT theories say, are full of people, congealed or 'dead labor' in Marxist terms, but as Abbott

(2005b) points out people often last longer than devices and their memories and knowledge can exceed what things can store or represent.

Devices are also embedded in people, then, and without forgetting that people are networked, far-from-equilibrium systems, we can understand some organizational changes, whatever the public narratives used to legitimize them, as emergent in a back and forth process in which the devices we make, becoming elements of our environments and articulations with the world, remake us.

Note

1. Both cases are presented schematically, with much of the story omitted. I once attempted to co-author a paper with B that would situate her work ethnographically in the local politics and parental advocacy around special education, but she complained that my writing gave her a headache. I hope this version is less painful.

References

Abbott, A. (2005a) The Idea of Outcome, in: G. Steinmetz (ed.), *The Politics of Method in the Human Sciences* (Durham, NC, Duke University Press)

Abbott, A. (2005b) The Historicality of Individuals, *Social Science History*, 29, pp. 1–13.

Association for Educational Communications and Technology. Official webpage available at: http://www.aect.org/About/History

B (1992) *One Child's Use of Assistive Technology*. Doctoral Dissertation.

Barley, S. (1996) Technicians in the Workplace: Ethnographic evidence for bringing work into organization studies, *Administrative Science Quarterly*, 41, pp. 404–441.

Barron, C. (ed.) (2003) A Strong Distinction Between Humans and Non-Humans is No Longer Required for Research Purposes: A debate between Bruno Latour and Steve Fuller, *History of the Human Sciences*, 16:2, pp. 77–99.

Barry, A. (1999) Demonstrations: Sites and sights of direct action, *Economy and Society*, 28, pp. 75–94.

Bechky, B. (2003) Object Lessons: Workplace artifacts as representations of occupational jurisdiction, *American Journal of Sociology*, 109, pp. 720–752.

Berg, M. & Akrich, M. (2004) Introduction—Bodies on Trial: Performances and politics in medicine and biology, *Body & Society*, 10, pp. 1–12.

Berkman, D. (1977) Instructional Television: The medium whose future has passed, in: J. Ackerman & L. Lipsitz (eds), *Instructional television: Status and directions* (Englewood Cliffs, NJ, Educational Technology Publications).

Bijker, W. (2007) Dikes and Dams, Thick With Politics, *Isis*, 98, pp. 109–123

Braverman, H. (1974) *Labor and Monopoly Capital* (New York, Monthly Review Press).

Callon, M. (1991) Techno-economic Networks and Irreversibility, in: J. Law (ed.), *A Sociology of Monsters: Essays on power, technology and domination* (London & New York, Routledge), pp. 132–161.

Callon, M. (2005) Why Virtualism Paves the Way to Political Impotence: A reply to Daniel Miller's critique of *The Laws of the Markets*, *Economic Sociology: The European Electronic Newsletter*, 6:2, pp. 3–20. Available at: http://econsoc.mpifg.de/archive/esfeb05.pdf

Callon, M. & Law, J. (1995) Agency and the Hybrid *Collectif*, *The South Atlantic Quarterly*, 94, pp. 481–507.

Callon, M. & Law, J. (1997) After the Individual Iin Society: Lessons on collectivity from science, technology and society, *Canadian Journal of Sociology*, 22, pp. 165–182.

Comaroff, J. & Comaroff, J. (2001) On Personhood: An anthropological perspective from Africa, *Social Identities*, 7, pp. 267–283

Clark, A. & Fujimura, J. (1992) What Tools? Which jobs? Why right?, in: A. Clarke & J. Fujimura (eds), *The Right Tools for the Job: At work in Twentieth-Century Life Sciences* (Princeton, NJ, Princeton University Press).

Cooper, R. (1998) Assemblage Notes, in: R. Chia (ed.), *Organized Worlds* (London, Routledge), pp. 108–129.

Coser, L. (1974) *Greedy Institutions: Patterns of undivided commitment* (New York, The Free Press).

Csordas, T. (1993) Somatic Modes of Attention, *Cultural Anthropology*, 8, pp. 135–156.

Czarniawska, B. (2009) Emerging Institutions: Pyramids or anthills, *Organizational Studies*, 30, pp. 423–441.

Erevelles, N. (2002) (Im)material Citizens: Cognitive disability, race, and the politics of citizenship, *Disability, Culture and Education*, 1:1, pp. 5–25.

Ferm, U., Ahlsen, E. & Bjorck-Akesson, E. (2005) Conversational Topics between a Child with Complex Communication Needs and her Caregiver at Mealtime, *Augmentative and Alternative Communication*, 21, pp. 19–40.

Ferguson, J. (1990) *The Anti-politics Machine* (Minneapolis, MN, University of Minnesota Press).

Foucault, M. (1979) *Discipline and Punish* (New York, Vintage).

Fuchs, S. (2001) *Against Essentialism* (Cambridge, MA, Harvard University Press).

Fujimura, J. (1992) Crafting Science: Standardized packages, boundary objects, and 'translation', in: A. Pickering (ed.), *Science as Practice and Culture* (Chicago, University of Chicago Press).

Gallagher, S. (2005) *How the Body Shapes the Mind* (Oxford, Clarendon Press).

Goffman, E. (1978) Response Cries, *Language*, 54, pp. 787–815.

Goldbart, J. & Marshall, J. (2004) 'Pushes and Pulls' on the Parents of Children who Use AAC, *Augmentative and Alternative Communication*, 20, pp. 194–208.

Goodwin, C. (1994) Professional Vision, *American Anthropologist*, 96, pp. 606–633.

Goossens, C. (1989) Aided Communication Intervention Before Assessment: A Case Study of a Child with Cerebral Palsy, *AAC: Augmentative and Alternative Communication*, 5, pp. 14–26.

Grosz, E. (1994) *Volatile Bodies: Toward a corporeal feminism* (Bloomington, IN, Indiana University Press).

Hirschman, A. (1991) *The Rhetoric of Reaction* (Cambridge, MA, Belknap).

Hutchins, E. (1995) *Cognition in the Wild* (Cambridge, MA, MIT Press).

Ingold, T. (2000) *The Perception of the Environment: Essays on livelihood, dwelling and skill* (London, Routledge).

Jacobson, J. W., Mulick, J. A. & Schwartz, A. A. (1995) A History of Facilitated Communication: Science, pseudoscience, and antiscience, *American Psychologist*, 50, pp. 750–765.

Kelly, S. (2005) 'A Different Light': Examining impairment through parent narratives of childhood disability, *Journal of Contemporary Ethnography*, 34, pp. 180–205.

Kirsch, S. & Mitchell, D. (2004) The Nature of Things: Dead labor, nonhuman actors, and the persistence of Marxism, *Antipode*, 36, pp. 687–705.

Knorr-Cetina, K. (1979) Tinkering Toward Success: Prelude to a theory of scientific practice, *Theory and Society*, 8, pp. 347–376

Lang, A. (1993) Non-Cartesian Artefacts in Dwelling Activities: Steps towards a semiotic ecology, *The Quarterly Newsletter of the Laboratory of Comparative Human Cognition*, 15, pp. 87–96.

Latour, B. (1994) On Technical Mediation, *Common Knowledge*, 3, pp. 29–64

Latour, B. (1996a) *Aramis, or the Love of Technology* (Cambridge, MA, Harvard University Press).

Latour, B. (1996b) On Actor-network Theory: A few clarifications, *Soziale Welt*, 47, pp. 369–381.

Latour, B. (1999) On Recalling ANT, in: J. Law & J. Hassard (eds), *Actor Network and After* (Oxford, Blackwell).

Latour, B. (2005) *Reassembling the Social* (Oxford, Oxford University Press).

Lave, J. (1988) *Cognition in Practice* (Cambridge, Cambridge University Press).

Law, J. (1994) *Organizing Modernity* (Oxford, Blackwell).

Law, J. (2009) Actor Network Theory and Material Semiotics, in: B. Turner (ed.), *The New Blackwell Companion to Social Theory* (Malden, MA, Blackwell), pp. 141–158.

Law, J. & Callon, M. (1992) The Life and Death of an Aircraft: A network analysis of technical change, in: W. Bijker & J. Law (eds), *Shaping Technology/Building Society: Studies in sociotechnical change* (Cambridge, MA, MIT Press).

Law, J. & Singleton, V. (2000) Performing Technology's Stories: On social constructivism, performance, and performativity, *Technology and Culture*, 40, pp. 324–357.

Lee, C. (2007) Boundary Negotiating Artifacts: Unbinding the Routine of Boundary Objects and Embracing Chaos in Collaborative Work, *Computer Supported Cooperative Work*, 16, pp. 307–339

Merleau-Ponty, M. (1963) *The Primacy of Perception* (Evanston, IL, Northwestern University Press).

Mialet, H. (2003) Reading Hawking's Presence: An interview with the self-effacing man, *Critical Inquiry*, 29, pp. 571–598.

Moser, I. (2003) *Road Traffic Accidents: The ordering of subjects, bodies and disability* (Oslo, Unipub).

Munro, R. (1996) The Consumption View of Self: Extension, exchange and identity, in: S. Edgell, K. Hetherington & A. Warde (eds), *Consumption Matters* (Oxford, Blackwell).

Nespor, J. (2006) *Technology and the Politics of Instruction* (Mahwah, NJ, Erlbaum).

Nutch, F. (1996) Gadgets, Gizmos, and Instruments: Science for the tinkering, *Science, Technology, and Human Values*, 21, pp. 214–228.

Pierson, P. (2004) *Politics in Time: History, institutions, and social analysis* (Princeton, NJ, Princeton University Press).

Pinch, T., Collins, H. M. & Carbone, L. (1996) Inside Knowledge: Second order measures of skill, *The Sociological Review*, 44, pp. 163–186.

Shapin, S. & Schaffer, S. (1985) *Leviathan and the Air-pump: Hobbes, Boyle, and the experimental life* (Princeton, NJ, Princeton University Press).

Shilling, C. (2005) *The Body in Culture, Technology & Society* (London, Sage).

Singleton, V. & Michael, M. (1993) Actor-networks and Ambivalence: General practitioners in the UK Cervical Screening Programme, *Social Studies of Science*, 23, pp. 227–264.

Slaughter, S. (1993). Retrenchment in the 1980s: The politics of gender and prestige, *Journal of Higher Education*, 64, pp. 250–311.

Somers, M. & Block, F. (2005) From Poverty to Perversity, *American Sociological Review*, 70, pp. 260–287

Star, S. (1995) Introduction, in: S. L. Star (ed.), *Ecologies of Knowledge: Work and politics in science and technology* (Albany, NY, State University of New York Press).

Stone, A. (1995) *The War of Desire and Technology at the Close of the Mechanical Age* (Cambridge, MA, MIT Press).

Strauss, C. (2007) Blaming for Columbine: Conceptions of agency in the contemporary United States, *Current Anthropology*, 48, pp. 807–832.

Thomas, C. (2004) How is Disability Understood? An examination of sociological approaches, *Disability & Society*, 19, pp. 569–583.

Tilly, C. (2002) *Stories, Identities, and Political Change* (Lanham, MD, Rowman & Littlefield).

Winance, M. (2006) Trying Out the Wheelchair: The mutual shaping of people and devices through adjustment, *Science, Technology, & Human Values*, 31, pp. 52–72.

Zangari, C., Lloyd, L. & Vicker, B. (1994) Augmentative and Alternative Communication: An historic perspective, *AAC: Augmentative and Alternative Communication*, 10, pp. 27–59.

2
Translating the Prescribed into the Enacted Curriculum in College and School

RICHARD EDWARDS

> To translate is to betray: ambiguity is part of translation. (Latour, 1996, p. 48)

Introduction

Over the years, there has been much written on the differences and similarities in the curriculum as prescribed, described and enacted (Bloomer, 1997). There has also been much research into the factors that impact upon what happens as the curriculum is enacted. A simple heuristic identifies such factors as:

- contextual e.g. national policy, funding arrangements;
- organisational e.g. nature and size of institution and subject department, styles of management, level and type of resources, locus of decision-making, internal or external assessments;
- curriculum e.g. the ways in which the curriculum is prescribed, nature of the curriculum i.e. academic or vocational;
- micro-political e.g. collegial, hierarchical or individualistic, expectations of students and parents; and
- individual e.g. professional formation and dispositions of lecturers and teachers, student backgrounds and prior experiences.

However, what such approaches to understanding such issues can do is reify and black box the curriculum as a taken for granted object, bounded by a context which (mis)shapes it in unexpected ways (Edwards *et al.*, 2009). These factors can therefore be positioned as in some ways external to curriculum-making practices and explanatory of them. A possible further inference of issues being posed in this manner is that, if these factors could be controlled, then curriculum-making would be much improved. The emphasis here is on explanation, on *why* differences in the enacted curriculum occur, as the basis for exerting control over it. In the process, curriculum-making may be reduced to a set of explanatory factors and techniques.

Such approaches to understanding are part of wider theoretical tendencies to work with a foundationalist ontology and *a priori* distinctions as a means of practising knowledge. These distinctions, for example, inside-outside, subject-object, nature-culture,

Researching Education Through Actor-Network Theory, First Edition. Edited by Tara Fenwick and Richard Edwards.
Chapters © 2012 The Authors. Book compilation © 2012 Philosophy of Education Society of Australasia.

human-non-human, theory-practice, provide the basis for what I would call a disciplining enactment in research practices. An *a priori* asymmetry is built into such enactments, which produce explanations of the world which examine one thing in terms of the other and, through this, seek to order or discipline the world through human intentions and agency. It is these approaches that have been the subject of radical challenge from a number of quarters. In this article I will explore this challenge through some of the work loosely referred to as actor-network theory (ANT) or material semiotics (Fenwick & Edwards, 2010).

In ANT, a generalised symmetry is enacted in relation to different actors, whether animate or inanimate and approaches are adopted for 'levelling divisions usually taken to be foundational' (Law, 2007). In other words, there are no *a priori* distinctions in this approach. Here rather than reducing curriculum-making to a single ontology through explanation, its possible enactments are taken as multiple and heterogeneous, arising from the relating of the animate and inanimate in networks which have agentic effects (Mol, 2002). Instead of looking at the *factors* that can be positioned to explain differences between the prescribed, described and enacted curriculum to bring about their closer alignment, we need to examine more closely the *actors* in the multiplicity of curriculum-making practices (Fountain, 1999). The emphasis then is on describing closely *how* things come to be the case without privileging human intention and agency. I am arguing therefore that much of the current shape of debate around these issues is unhelpful, as it suggests a possibility precisely for control and prescription based upon *a priori* distinctions, which is unavailable due to the heterogeneity and multiplicity of practices.

This is where the concept of translation becomes helpful. Explanation and control are associated with a fantasy of *implementing* the prescribed curriculum in its enactments in a linear sense. Early writings on ANT propose that practices are translated, changed in the process of changing, betraying human intention. Factors impacting upon the curriculum may be real, but they are not foundational explanations and to enact them as such is to miss the point of the translations to which they are subject. In other words, despite the attempt at standardisation of learning outcomes in the prescribed curriculum, its uptake of individuals, artefacts and organisations is multiply enacted and incapable of control due to the practices of translation or betrayal (Mulcahy, 1998, 1999). Standardisation is therefore an (un)stable and precarious achievement. This article therefore argues for an alternative ontology to that which pervades much research through which to examine educational practices.

To explore this, I intend to draw upon certain aspects of actor-network theory and the data arising from one part of a research project which has sought to explore curriculum-making in three matched subjects in an upper secondary school and a further education college in a medium sized town in Scotland. The article is in four parts. First, I outline briefly the background to the empirical study. Second, I sketch those aspects of early actor-network theory upon which I draw and why I consider them helpful. Third, I provide two case studies of curriculum making in the subject of Hospitality. These case studies will illuminate the ways in which the prescribed curriculum in the form of unit descriptors—texts which inscribe the standards that students are meant to achieve—become (in)visible in the translations of the practices of curriculum-making and the people, spaces and artefacts that are translated in the process. In this way, I begin to explore how this theoretical work produces a different language of description in enacting educational practices. Finally I shall explore some of the inferences to be drawn for educational research and theory from the approach I am suggesting.

Background to the Study

Historically, in Scotland, schools focused on an academic curriculum, while colleges provided a more occupation-related curriculum (Bryce & Humes, 1999; Leech, 1999). This has changed, as some schools have sought to provide more occupationally-oriented opportunities for students for whom the academic curriculum may be less appropriate, while colleges have developed their provision of the higher level occupation-related curriculum and also academic opportunities for students (Thomson, 2003: Canning, 2007). The result is that currently parts of the curriculum are common to both schools and colleges. These changes impact upon curriculum coherence, transition and progression for students within the curriculum and between institutional contexts.

It is the outcomes-based Scottish Qualifications Authority (SQA) unit descriptors which schools and colleges mainly utilise when developing a curriculum in particular subjects. These provide the basis for the prescribed curriculum by specifying certain learning outcomes to be achieved at a specified level within a hierarchical system of assessment. At the level of the prescription therefore the curriculum is very standardised and rational, in principle enabling and supporting student mobility and the portability of credit within the education system. Such approaches are common around the world. In theory, there are many curriculum routes to achieve the outcomes and this provides the possibility for creative approaches to pedagogy on the part of institutions, departments and teachers/lecturers (Higham, 2003). It is such possibilities that are often represented in the described curriculum (Bloomer, 1997), those often idealised narratives of practice provided by teachers, lecturers and students. This approach assumes that learning outcomes are the same despite different contexts for and means of developing and demonstrating them.

However, research evidence suggests that there is less diversity in the described and enacted curriculum than envisioned or desired (Smyth *et al.*, 1998). Indeed many unit descriptors would seem to seek greater standardisation, as they do not only specify learning outcomes, but also make broad statements about expectations in relation to teaching, learning and assessment practices to achieve those goals, thereby seeming to limit the possibilities for diversity. Further, a great deal of research points to a tendency for continuity rather than change in what goes on in schools and colleges in response to centrally mandated reform initiatives (e.g. Spillane, 1999; Goodson, 2004). Cuban (1984) identified a number of stability factors in schools that militate against changes in practice, for example, schools prize obedience over independent thinking, the existing culture of teaching, and the socialisation of teachers through their own schooling. The availability of published textbooks and other resources, and teachers' existing frames of reference also act to enable and constrain curriculum-making in certain ways. Bates (1989) stressed the importance of teachers' material, especially career interests, in determining how new initiatives are mediated. Daniels (2001) refers to 'stuck' and 'moving' schools to contrast those in which teachers are less willing to take risks and those where this is not the case. While most of the existing studies focus on curriculum-making in schools, these factors are also relevant in curriculum-making in the college context also (James & Biesta, 2007).

Such factors and the persistence of established practices are positioned as contributing to the gaps between the prescribed, described and the enacted curriculum, despite the supposed standardisation imposed through prescription. The research thus suggests that attempts to provide a standardised prescribed curriculum with equivalences across sites is not being achieved in the enacted curriculum. Different questions can be inferred from this conclusion. As I have said, research has tended to focus on trying to provide explanatory factors for such divergence, with curriculum-making being taken as an object to be explained with the potential for future control and stabilisation. In this article, I am exploring a different tack, which assumes that difference and multiplicity is inherent in curriculum-making practices and therefore there is nothing to be explained as such. It is simply the case. This raises questions about the helpfulness of examining curriculum-making drawing upon the typology of the prescribed, described and enacted as it has largely been taken up (Bloomer, 1997). I will return to this in the final section of this article.

The data, upon which the remainder of this article draws, were generated in two associated sites, a secondary school (Woodland Academy) and a college of further education (Riverside College). The project explored three curriculum areas, drawing data from various SQA courses at equivalent levels between the two sites. These were Hospitality, Life Sciences and Technical Studies. They have been taken as *telling* cases; having significance beyond the particular circumstances of the case. Each unit within the individual curriculum areas had similar learning outcomes specified in the prescribed curriculum. The students on each unit were all aged 16–18. This was to enable as close a comparison across organisational sites as possible. Data were derived from existing documents, and cycles of classroom observations and interviews with staff and students on the selected units over the course of one term in the autumn of 2007. These have been subject to descriptive interpretation to produce detailed case studies and thematic analysis for cross site comparison. Pseudonyms have been used for the school and college, and for individuals to protect the anonymity of respondents. In this article, I only draw upon the data from the Hospitality units.

Actor-Network Theory

At one level, to say I am drawing upon actor-network theory (ANT) is a bit of a misnomer, given that there is no established body of theory and indeed many of the major proponents associated with ANT would refute the notion of a stable body of theory as they have at times refuted the term ANT itself (Law & Hassard, 1999). Different strands of theorising are therefore entangled in and around the notion of ANT. Further many of the key texts identified under the umbrella of ANT are highly detailed ethnographies of scientific and technological practices and innovations. While ANT has been taken up in a range of other social sciences, there has been relatively little uptake in education research (e.g. Roth & McGinn, 1998; Fountain 1999; Fenwick & Edwards,

2010). A small literature has developed over the last fifteen years but it is somewhat piecemeal. One reason for this relative lack of engagement with ANT may be the challenge to education as a human-centred practice that is at its heart. ANT seeks to develop analyses that do not rely upon the *a priori* distinctions that shape many of our understandings and practices. Drawing upon a principle of symmetry, ANT derived analysis seeks to explore phenomenon as a form of heterogeneous engineering, in which the human and non-human are treated as of equal importance in enacting practices. Assumed foundational distinctions between for example, the social and natural, the material and cultural are eschewed in this approach. 'ANT avoids the problem of naturalisation (i.e. scientific rationality), socialisation (i.e. social constructivism or cognition), and textualisation (i.e. deconstruction)' (Fountain, 1999, p. 343). The practices through which distinctions and objects are enacted and become taken for granted or 'black boxed' becomes something to be studied.

ANT is understood as a diverse domain of conceptual and empirical work that explores how the people, objects, practices and ideas come to be organized and ordered in particular ways, while resisting its own authority as yet another reductionist theory. Law (2007) refers to ANT as a disparate set of:

> ... tools, sensibilities and methods of analysis that treat everything in the social and natural worlds as a continuously generated effect of the webs of relations within which they are located. It assumes that nothing has reality or form outside the enactment of those relations.

Here action is not an outcome of human intent but an effect of the mobilising of networks, a joint exercise of relational strategies within networks that are spread across space and time and performed through inanimate—e.g. books, journals, pens, computers, unit descriptors, pots, pans—as well as animate objects in precarious arrangements. Here order and stability are temporary network effects and not inherent in materials or objects. Unlike most framings therefore, ANT does not privilege human consciousness or intention. Both the animate and inanimate are treated as materially equal. The symmetry between inanimate and animate objects in ANT arises because 'human powers increasingly derive from the complex *interconnections* of humans with material objects ... . This means that the human and physical worlds are elaborately intertwined and cannot be analysed separate from each other' (Urry, 2000, p. 14). For Law (2007), the discussion of ANT as solely theory misses the point, as 'theory is embedded and extended in empirical practice and practice itself is necessarily theoretical'. It is for this reason that as an approach—and it is not singular—ANT is descriptive of how things happen through the growth and shrinking of networks rather than attempting to explain them based upon foundational causes. It is itself enacted through empirical case studies and attempts to show rather than tell.

An early formulation of ANT identified four moments of translation in the establishment of a network (Callon, 1986): problematisation; interessement, enrolment and mobilisation. Problematisation is about what subjectivities and interests are allowable within specific networks—the inclusions and exclusions. Defining the problem therefore acts as a powerful form of gatekeeping. 'Interessement' identifies the practices through which barriers are built between that which is part of the network and that which is not.

'These can be material barriers ... , material organisations of space and time that restrict contact with outsiders ... , discursive barriers ... , or barriers constituted through differences of taste, style and language' (Nespor, 1994, p. 14). They are the relations through which actors are enticed away from other networks and other interests are excluded. While interessement sets the barriers to participation, enrolment fashions the alliances within the network. Mobilisations are the practices through which enrolled networks are stabilised, however temporarily, and made manageable and mobile. 'Techniques can range from mobilisation in the flesh—assembling strikers for a mass rally, for example, or translating students into mobile practitioners of a discipline—to the representation of previously dispersed entities in stable, mobile, and combinable forms (textual or electronic)' (Nespor, 1994, p. 14).

In relation to curriculum-making, we might therefore say that it is itself multiply ordered, assembled, distributed and enacted through a range of material semiotic networks within which any object is interconnected, linked to institutional structures, everyday practices, and policies in different domains. In particular, curriculum-making can be traced in the processes of assembling and maintaining these networks, as well as in the negotiations and translations that occur at and within various nodes comprising a network. In this approach:

> ... the meanings of an event are constituted by hooking it up to moving networks of people acting, with, through, and by virtue of their entanglements with durable artefacts, structures and materials. Into these networks of action are woven so many commitments, identities and interests ... (Nespor, 2003, p. 95)

ANT emphasises the enacted nature of practices, as 'left to their own devices *human actions and words do not spread very far at all*' (Law, 1994, p. 24, emphasis in original).

These enactments are the translations through which networks form, reform and dissolve.

> According to the latter [the model of translation], the spread in time and space of anything—claims, orders, artefacts, goods—is in the hands of people; each of these people may act in many different ways, letting the token drop, or modifying it, or deflecting it, or betraying it, or adding to it, or appropriating it ... . When no one is there to take up the statement or token then it simply drops. (Latour, 1986, p. 267)

Without such practices, there is no network. ANT therefore emphasises the changing nature of human knowledge and practices and the actions through which power is exercised. However, translation is never a straight forward process; 'translation is always insecure, a process susceptible to failure. Disorder—or other orders—are only precariously kept at bay' (Law, 2007).

The role of the token is important here. In early ANT, a token can be both discourses and objects. Latour (1987) used the notion of token to challenge more conventional views that ideas and objects diffuse through society. In this latter view, the idea or object is unchanged by its movement within the social realm. The token remains itself. As Gaskell and Hepburn (1998, p. 66) explain it, in a diffusion approach,

> ... once 'discovered' or 'invented', the token moves through society unchanged
> encountering either people who use it and pass it on to others or people who
> resist it and don't use it. The path of the token is a product of the power of the
> originator of the idea and the frictions and resistances (lack of communication,
> ill will, opposition from interest groups, indifference) that it encounters.

The concept of translation provides us with an alternative way of understanding these
movements across space and time. Here a token is usually not passed unchanged, but can
be ignored or taken up and translated as different interests are invested in it. As a result,
the token is itself changed.

> The path of the token is a product of the number and strength of the links that
> are established between it and a diverse group of other actors. It is not a
> product of an initial quality but of the subsequent actions of a multitude of
> others. In the model of translation, not only the token is continuously trans-
> formed as links with other actors are established but so are the other actors. As
> they take up and use the token, their actions and patterns of practice are
> changed as they see new possibilities with the token. Those associated with the
> token form a network through links with the token. The network is defined by
> the token but the token is also simultaneously defined by the network. The
> network and token co-evolve. As the token/network system stabilises the token
> is seen to be an unproblematic artefact or to define a part of nature, the
> network is seen to define a part of society and each is dependent on the other.
> (Gaskell & Hepburn, 1998, p. 66)

These translations are possible because tokens are always unfinished and there are
patterns of possibility that can be inscribed into them and that they inscribe in others.

The co-emergence of token and network is precisely an actor-network. Here the
changes that emerge across space and time are not a problem to be explained, as we see
in much of the discussion about the differences between the prescribed, described and
enacted curriculum. It is rather an expected part of curriculum-making as a set of
practices. As practices, curriculum-making is an enactment which is inevitably multiple
both across different networks of action but also for those engaged in the practices.

How then to represent this? In their study, Gaskell and Hepburn (1998) explored the
way in which a particular curriculum innovation in Canada was translated in different
ways in two settings to establish what they refer to as a 'coursenetwork'. They follow the
official prescribed curriculum for the course innovation into the settings. This was based
upon sets of inscriptions through which the innovation became visible as text. It is such
inscriptions that become 'immutable mobiles' in the translations at play, functioning as
'objects of professional conversation ... tools to coordinate those professional conversations ... and as boundaries between and coordinates within those communities of practice' (Fountain, 1999, p. 346). Gaskell and Hepburn (1998, p. 74) use such ideas to
follow the translations of the curriculum change they studied.

> By focusing on the course as a token circulating and simultaneously defining
> and being defined by a network, and seeing the outcome as a coursenetwork,
> it is possible to understand the construction of different outcomes. An inno-

vation tests the strength of the links in an existing coursenetwork. A successful innovation results in a modification to that coursenetwork. The stability of the innovation increases as the number of human and non-human actors linked to the innovation increases and as the strength of those links increases. However, the successful enrolment of additional actors entails translating their interests into the course through a process of negotiation in which the course and the actors are simultaneously transformed.

While many of the early concepts from ANT have undergone critique and development (Law & Hassard, 1999; Latour, 2005; Law, 2007), it remains important to examine the work they can do in particular circumstances—to mobilise them in the enactment of research and enactment as research.

The Prescribed Curriculum: An (In)visible Token?

In this section I draw upon the data to construct two short descriptive case studies of curriculum-making in Hospitality. Drawing on the principle of symmetry and the concepts of translation and token, I am particularly interested in the unit descriptor, representing the prescribed curriculum, as token in this process. The unit descriptors are themselves an effect of a lot of work to stabilise and bound a set of activities as standardised 'learning outcomes' that can then be taken up within different educational settings. Inscription is part of that process and also their authoritative location in an online library of units and qualification at the SQA. Their virtuality means that they are an outcome of the translation of a QWERTY keyboard into code, which can then be retrieved online or in print as written text. Their availability is distributed across space and time, in order to regulate through the standardisation of learning outcomes.

The college Hospitality unit descriptor—Cookery Processes—had as its prescribed outcomes:

> Describe the cookery processes, their associated principles, and foods suitable for each process.
> Perform numerical tasks related to food preparation.
> Using commercial catering equipment, carry out the cookery processes to given specifications.
> Interpret oral instructions and standard recipes to carry out the cookery processes on a range of foods.

The school Hospitality unit descriptor—Practical Skills for the Hospitality Industry—had as its prescribed outcomes:

> Prepare a range of food using appropriate techniques and equipment.
> Cook and present a range of food to an appropriate standard.
> Work in a safe and hygienic manner.

The similarity in the two units is emphasised by a certain commonality in the more detailed expectations of teaching, learning and assessment activities associated with the descriptors. Both of these tokens therefore focused on enabling students to prepare food in a safe and hygienic way using appropriate equipment and techniques. In order so to do, they needed to mobilise a variety of people and artefacts in particular settings in order that they have an existence.

Both units were part of courses with very similar overall aims. The college course—Professional Cookery—aimed to provide 'a thorough introduction to the techniques, skills and knowledge required to operate in the kitchen areas of a wide variety of commercial establishments'. The school course—Practical Cookery—aimed to provide 'the development of techniques and skills required for food production appropriate to domestic and hospitality situations'. The difference between the two courses is in the way in which the home is mobilised as a setting for hospitality as well as commercial settings. The SQA provide these two courses with a slightly different emphasis and balance between the aims and learning outcomes. The course and the unit descriptors therefore attempt to translate different organisational sites through the expression of foci more closely allied with the interests of those organisations. Schools have traditionally had a 'home economics' focus to what they do, while colleges are more focused on preparing students for occupations in hospitality. The institutions can ostensibly 'choose' which course at this level is most appropriate to their own organisational aims and best suited to their staff and student profiles. However, the tokens make themselves more available to one setting rather than the other through the ways in which they inscribe the outcomes to be achieved.

The cases below are illustrative only, both attempting to give some indication of the detail necessary in formulating an ANT empirical account of curriculum-making, but also indicating the range of actors that are heterogeneously engineered to produce what is often taken to be the black box of the curriculum. For space reasons, these illustrations are not the full ethnographies that ANT would ideally require. However, this notion is itself a misnomer, as at some point all networks have to be cut in order to say anything at all (Strathern, 1996). The short cases attempt to illuminate curriculum-making as network effects, in the process showing how similar unit descriptors (tokens) acted as inscriptions and were translated into different coursenets as the prescribed curriculum was enacted in the different settings.

The College Setting: Hospitality—Cookery Processes

In the college, the unit descriptor mobilised and was translated by the lecturer, Malcolm, an ex-professional chef with many years experience of different kitchens, who had gained his occupational qualifications part-time. His enrolment into full-time lecturing at college was gradual and importantly influenced by personal reasons, in particular the desire for more family-friendly working hours. Prior to becoming a lecturer, Malcolm had worked in Edinburgh, Glasgow, Aberdeen, Stirling and in Holland. He moved into tutoring while working in a restaurant, initially one day per week, thereby both extending his initial networks but also practising the interessement between the two networks of the restaurant and the college. He then obtained a one year temporary contract as a lecturer. His enthusiasm for restaurant work was broad-based, not least the multiculturalism of the workplace—'people from different walks and different cultures'. While working, he was given the opportunity to gain teaching qualifications in the late 1990s. His approach to teaching could therefore be said to model forms of workplace apprenticeship and it was this that enabled the token to translate and be translated into a particular form of the enacted curriculum, what is being referred to here as the hospitality coursenet. He therefore does, as Mulcahy (1998, p. 28) found in her research on vocational education:

> Switching between, and combining, the tools and materials of competency-based training (for example, textual representations of competency; pre-set standards) and the tools and materials of their practice worlds (for instance, bodily representations of competency; negotiated standards; 'process' approaches to curricula).

The unit was taught over 2 lots of 18 weeks, with three kitchen-based sessions and one classroom-based session per week. Attendance by students was erratic—Malcolm identified 1 or 2 of the nine students as 'not good attendees', their enrolment into the coursenet being incomplete. The unit descriptor was translated within the college in three adjacent spaces—a large kitchen, a small kitchen and a more conventional class-room. The kitchens simulated the environments to be found in commercial hospitality workplaces. Each of these spaces was mobilised at different times for different purposes. A lot of the work in the kitchens involved preparing food for the college restaurant which was open to the public. The interests of the public's desire for food and the standards of the industry therefore had to be enrolled into the ways in which the token was enacted in the practices of Malcolm and the students.

Malcolm initially taught the students by focusing on building up their basic skills in cooking. When they reached a certain level, they then started prepping the food for the restaurant, the interests of the customers being used to shape the practices of the kitchen. Later in the year, they moved on to preparing and cooking the menus for the restaurant. The professional orientation of this enactment was embodied in the clothes of staff and students when working in the kitchens—white coats, hats, and trousers. This wear was provided to students at the start of their course, along with knives and a Cookery Book that had all the information they needed to pass the assessment for the unit. The Cookery Book inscribed the outcomes of the unit descriptor, but translated them to embrace the full range of knowledge, understanding and recipes which were required. The enactments in the kitchens meant there was a lot of noise, heat and movement. The token was translated into the activities associated with working in this occupation, but also became invisible, as references were to the Cookery Book and not the unit descriptor itself. The Cookery Book therefore became a key actor in curriculum-making, a focus for activity that brought together the lecturer, students, artefacts and ingredients to rehearse the practices of commercial hospitality kitchens.

However, as there were also more conventional educational outcomes to be achieved, the unit descriptor also mobilised certain artefacts from the conventional classroom within the kitchens. Flipchart and text books, which would not be in a commercial setting, were enrolled in the coursenet. The flipchart displayed the menu the students were working on and the number of portions needed. The text books were open and the students followed instructions on food preparation from Malcolm. There was also a folder with the recipes for the restaurant menus. The students moved between using the recipes for large numbers of customers from the folder and the precise instructions around processes for smaller numbers found in the text book. There was thus an immense textual mediation of the curriculum, which was perhaps unexpected given that Hospitality is an arena often associated with limited literacy (Ivanic *et al.*, 2009).

The classroom was laid out with student tables forming a rectangle, with the lecturer at the front, a particular ordering space and possibilities for interaction. A range of artefacts was available in the space to be mobilised. There included a digital screen, audio-visual equipment and an Over Head Projector which sat on the lecturer's desk. As well as class-related items on their desks, the students often had mobile phones, drinks and iPods visible, giving a certain informality to the atmosphere, translating their interests as individuals and not merely as students into the curriculum space. This could be seen as undermining the strength of the coursenet, but in this situation seemed to enhance it by recognising the students as more than students. This informality contrasted with the formality of their work in the kitchens which needed to be clutter free of personal items for health and safety reasons. This change in activity and use of space was also signalled through a more chatty style which punctuated the more focused instructional discourse of the classroom interactions. In the kitchen the whole focus was on the food preparation and any talk between teacher and students tended to be about or related to the task in hand—the discipline of the task. This points to the ways in which, in this case, a networked framing of curriculum-making points to the differences even within a single curriculum space and also how at certain times the network may be more or less open.

Malcolm's approach to his teaching resulted in an invisibility to the token that which was being translated. He tried to embed the teaching of core skills into the subject curriculum and did not over-emphasise assessment. The unit descriptor was translated into the Cookery Book which was the pivotal text through which the students' practices developed. His approach could be termed practice-led, as he was keen to support the development of the working practices necessary for the occupation with which he had strong and ongoing links. Through Malcolm the unit descriptor and students were translated into the occupation of hospitality, resulting is a contextualising of the curriculum beyond the content inscribed in the token. He therefore emphasised the social aspects of becoming a chef in needing to develop the networks within the profession. Outside speakers from the hospitality industry were therefore brought in to talk with students and Malcolm encouraged his students to have part-time jobs in hospitality while studying. Here there was a clear attempt to mobilise dispositions and practices that would stand the students in good stead beyond the course. In this way the hospitality coursenet was expanded in order to make it more durable.

In the large kitchen, people and artefacts were mobilised in a number of ways, for instance, learning by doing by the students and demonstrating techniques by Malcolm. In the early sessions, this was a staged process within the session. As the unit progressed, Malcolm spent less time demonstrating. When not demonstrating, he walked around the kitchen, observing and commenting on students' work. He was also assessing, but this seemed to be a relatively unobtrusive activity, as not all the students were aware it was taking place. Malcolm described himself as assessing through observing and giving the students feedback, but this did not seem to reflect what was enacted. Malcolm also timed assessment to take place later in the unit, once students had had time to practice the tasks against which they were to be assessed. Thus while the token inscribed certain expectations around assessment, the practices mobilised through them, as well as the token itself, were relatively invisible.

A later session in the large kitchen was very buzzy, with much more of the feel of a commercial kitchen. The students were doing preparation for Christmas dinners in the restaurant and a second lecturer was working with Malcolm. Here the annual celebration was mobilised as the rationale for a particular set of recipes. Both lecturers were involved in demonstrating food preparation and asking short questions for students to answer. The students used their text books to guide them and there was less demonstrating than previously. Here the lecturer became less central to the working of the coursenet, as students referred to texts and each other in order to coordinate their activities. The importance of team work in a kitchen was emphasised. The students were encouraged to use the full range of their senses in food preparation—smell, taste, look, etc.—and reminded that aspects of cooking are to do with personal preference in terms of taste. Here the embodied experience of food was mobilised as a way through which students could learn. Malcolm went around giving advice, instructions and encouragement. He recognised the greater intensity—'it's to give the guys a little bit of a push'. This was based on the increased scale of cooking for large numbers compared to the smaller number of portions prepared at the start of the unit.

The translations of certain parts of the token into *theory* proved the most problematic. Classroom-based sessions were translated as theory and, for the students, were the least favoured part of the course—'it's the theory work that's kind of difficult I find ... I'm not really managing it very well' (Bob). The material practices associated with theory—reading, speaking, and writing—were contrasted with those of the kitchen. While the work of the kitchen enrolled the students, that of the classroom did not. It is not that theory does not involve practices in their own right, but it was the translation of those practices into and by the students that was the issue. Students struggled to translate the practices of theory in ways which were not the case with engaging in tasks in the kitchen. Theory sessions were contrasted with practical sessions rather being positioned as entailing certain practices in their own right. This was one of the fractures in the hospitality coursenet.

The students in this group were diverse in terms of age and background. Most had some previous or current affiliation to cooking. A number identified themselves as having not enjoyed school and been disruptive, yet they seemed focussed and working hard in the sessions observed. Their enrolment within the curriculum-making of this coursenet can be contrasted with their lack of enrolment in the coursenets of schooling. It would seem that their interests were being translated more successfully in this coursenet and, as a result, issues of behaviour and discipline did not have to become visible.

We therefore see that the token, the unit descriptor, takes up and is taken up in a networked array of material semiotic practices in enacting hospitality in curriculum-making in college. It therefore becomes a hospitality coursenet. This points to learning being not only about learners and teachers, but also about objects, spaces, texts. It also points to the fractures, incompleteness and multiple entanglements in curriculum-making.

The School Setting: Practical Cookery Skills for the Hospitality Industry

This unit descriptor in the school was translated by and translated Pauline as a teacher of Home Economics. She had started a degree in Food, Health and Welfare and, following a brief placement in a school, decided to become a teacher. She trained at University and then obtained a temporary post at the school in which she taught. Her practical experience of Hospitality was domestic rather than commercial and this was reflected in how she was mobilised in the enactment of the curriculum. It was domestic scales which were translated into the learning outcomes of this token. The hospitality industry became largely erased in the translations from the prescribed into the enacted curriculum. Here then, despite similar learning outcomes to those of the college unit, a cookery coursenet was enacted.

The unit descriptor was translated in one room in the Home Economics department of the school. The department was on the second floor and the corridor was full of posters promoting healthy eating and the smell of food and cooking pervaded. The classroom was divided into many kitchenette areas with a sink, oven, cupboards to store equipment and a work surface. The doors of the cupboards had diagrams on them to show what should be stored there. There was a walk-in cupboard at the front of the class which held fridge freezers and large containers. The scale was domestic rather than commercial, as were the number of portions of food the students produced. The kitchen combined as a classroom with a teacher's desk at the front with a digital board. There was a rotating white board also. The computer in the classroom was used by Pauline to display the learning outcomes of that class, to access emails and the like, but also to search the internet for information. The display of the learning outcomes made the token both translated but also very visible in each class. This display was central to the mobilising of activities in the coursenet.

However, the translation process also meant that certain aspects of the unit descriptor became invisible. Thus the full title of the unit was only placed on the inside cover of the teacher's workbook. On all other school produced materials e.g. student workbook and support notes and the recipe booklet, the unit was simply called *Practical Cookery*. This, alongside the scale of cookery in the class, suggests the occupational relevance of the unit was untranslated or pushed to one side by more powerful interests. As it was her first time of teaching the unit, Pauline worked entirely from the school produced packs, which, like Malcolm's Cookery Book, was mobilised as a translation of the unit descriptor into the classroom setting. Such packs themselves become tokens, the translations that brought them into enactment and the erasure of the hospitality industry being glossed over. Indeed the hospitality industry is black boxed and excluded through the silencing of this aspect in the unit descriptor as it is translated.

There were four students for this class, all female. Two were very interested in Home Economics, while the other two were doing the course more as a respite from their more academic studies. This contrasting enrolment was reflected in attendance, degrees of interest and the interactions of the teacher with the respective students. The small class contrasted with an equivalent class in the school, which had 18 students. The different size of groups arose from timetable issues within the school, the timetable being a major actor in the coursenet in terms of ordering people into specific spaces at certain times.

For Pauline, the small group allowed for a more informal and interactive style of teaching than normal. Ostensibly this might have supported strong enrolment within the coursenet but this did not occur, reflecting the different degrees of interessement of the students. Those with an interest in pursuing Home Economics beyond school were enrolled more strongly than those for whom it was positioned as a break from their main academic focus.

The unit descriptor translated Pauline who placed the learning outcomes for each class on the digital board. She went over them with the class. The scale of the servings was small—four. Because of the constraints of the timetable, not all aspects of the processes being engaged with were contained within the one class. The working within time frames of the hospitality coursenet was contrasted with the constant running out of time in the cookery coursenet.

In a further class, the equipment had been laid out in advance for the students. The two highly enrolled students entered first and moved straight into doing things. The learning outcomes were visible on the screen and the students had the recipe books out as a point of reference. The two less enrolled students arrived and were told by Pauline to 'get prepped'. The students got on with things and Pauline walked up and down being fairly informal and chatty, but keeping them on task, which the students seemed to like. She seemed to struggle with one of the less enrolled students who was particularly slow and appeared not much interested.

Pauline made very visible the assessment aspects of the Unit, reminding the students they had an assessment coming up and suggesting they take home worksheets, which were normally kept in the back of the classroom, in order to revise. Time seemed a fairly constant actor in trying to translate the unit descriptor in the curriculum. For instance, when the students were making cakes, Pauline instructed them to whisk the cream with an electric mixer once the cakes were in the oven. In principle, they should not use the electric whisk for this task but time was short. Pauline had the students set timers for the cakes (which ended up burning), and the students washed up and put away equipment. There was an even greater sense of hurriedness to this session than previous ones.

The final observed class focused on decorating and presenting food rather than preparing it. This entailed translating aesthetic sensibilities into the curriculum. The students had made shortbread and puree in the previous session. Pauline demonstrated the combining of puree with cream to form the filling for the shortbread and explained how the property of icing sugar enables it to set. She instructed them to wipe down surfaces and choose a garnish. While the students were wiping down surfaces, Pauline did a drawing on the whiteboard of her proposed display of food on the plate providing a visualisation of that to be enacted. She gave the students a range of ideas for displays but said it was their choice how they did it.

She gathered the students around and demonstrated the decorating of the plate she had drawn. Pauline involved the students in making the decisions about what would look good as she did this. The students did their own designs and Pauline helped them to finish these. She had the students show their finished displays to the Principal Teacher, who was also very positive about them. One student took a photo of the design on her mobile phone. Pauline gave them permission to taste one of the desserts, after which they washed up.

Once again, in this example we witness how a large network is translated by and translates the token of the unit descriptor as it enters a particular site. By contrast with the hospitality coursenet in the college example, the school example can be characterised as a cookery coursenet. We also witness how ostensibly similar learning outcomes are enacted multiply through the translations to which the unit descriptors are subject, mobilising different spaces, people and artefacts as curriculum-making.

Inferences

It is clear that any notion of implementation or diffusion in the enactment of the curriculum is misplaced, given the range and diversity of the interests, identities and artefacts, as tokens are translated and translate, betrayed and betray. The case studies clearly indicate the ways in which the token of the prescribed curriculum is translated as it mobilises and is itself translated by a range of other actors in the network. The prescribed curricula are enacted as a hospitality and cookery coursenet respectively. This cannot be reduced simply to human intention, or other factors as foundational explanations of what is occurring. Similar prescribed learning outcomes result in very different types of educative enactments. In the process, the prescribed curriculum in its translations has varying degrees of visibility as it is enacted. Curriculum-making is heterogeneous and multiple from this anti-foundationalist ontology positioning and not an object within a context.

Although ostensibly taking similar units within a standardised curriculum framework, it is clear that the enacted curriculum in Hospitality varies significantly as it is translated into the different settings of school and college. We may infer from this one case that schools and colleges may provide similar opportunities at a formal level, but they are very different organisations serving different student groups, often with different types of staff with varying professional backgrounds and formations. Curriculum-making is multiple precisely because the prescribed curriculum mobilises different networks of actors. Thus, as Mulcahy (1999, p. 97) suggests, lecturers and teachers engage in a 'strategic juggling of representational ambiguity' among the varied standards inscribed in the prescribed curriculum of unit descriptors and the like. Difference and multiplicity in the curriculum is therefore to be expected and described rather than be identified as problematic and explained (away). This raises important educational questions about the status and equivalence of learning outcomes within a standardised curriculum and the type and amount of work that is necessary to exclude multiplicity in the name of standardisation.

We may therefore need to begin to reframe some of our research focus from examining factors to explain differences to exploring actors enacting those differences through symmetry, translation and other concepts from actor-network theory. To examine curriculum-making as a network effect in which no *a priori* status is given to certain objects is not an easy thing to grasp, or to represent adequately. What it does point to is that there is more to curriculum-making than we might imagine and that what is enrolled and translated into it makes a big difference in terms of both practices and what is learnt. This also goes beyond cognitive and social understandings of the curriculum, both of which are based on the search for foundational explanations. This may not be a comfortable space, but it is a necessary one if we are to make sense of the curriculum-making practices in education.

Acknowledgments

This article is based on a research project, Cultures of Curriculum-Making in School and College, funded by the ESRC (RES -000-22-2452). My thanks to my colleagues Kate Miller and Mark Priestley, with whom I worked on the project and to the staff and students that made it all possible.

References

Bates, I. (1989) Versions of Vocationalism: An analysis of some social and political influences on curriculum policy and practice, *British Journal of Sociology of Education*, 10:2, pp. 215–231.

Bloomer, M. (1997) *Curriculum Making in Post-16 Education* (London, Routledge).

Bryce, T. & Humes, W. (1999) Scottish Secondary Education: Philosophy and practice, in: T. Bryce & W. Humes (eds), *Scottish Education* (Edinburgh, Edinburgh University Press).

Callon, M. (1986) Some Elements of a Sociology of Translation: Domestication of the scallops and the fishermen, in: J. Law (ed.), *Power, Action and Belief: A new sociology of knowledge* (London, Routledge and Kegan Paul).

Canning, R. (2007) A History of Core Skills Development Policy in Scotland, *Scottish Educational Review*, 39:2, pp. 138–147.

Cuban, L. (1984) *How Teachers Taught: Constancy and change in American classrooms 1890–1980* (New York, Teachers College Press).

Daniels, H. (2001) *Vygotsky and Pedagogy* (London, Routledge).

Edwards, R., Biesta, G. & Thorpe, M. (eds) (2009) *Rethinking Contexts for Learning and Teaching: Communities, activities and networks* (London, Routledge).

Fenwick, T. & Edwards, R. (2010) *Actor-Network Theory and Education* (London, Routledge).

Fountain, R-M. (1999) Socio-scientific Issues via Actor Network Theory, *Journal of Curriculum Studies*, 31:3, pp. 339–58.

Gaskell, J. & Hepburn, G. (1998) The Course as Token: A construction of/by networks, *Research in Science Education*, 28:1, pp. 65–76.

Goodson, I. F. (2004) Understanding Curriculum Change: Some warnings about restructuring initiatives, in: F. Hérnandez & I. Goodson (eds), *Social Geographies of Educational Change* (London, Kluwer Academic Publishers).

Higham, J. J. S. (2003) Curriculum Change: A study of the implementation of general national vocational qualifications, *The Curriculum Journal*, 14:3, pp. 317–340.

Ivanic, R., Edwards, R., Barton, D., Martin-Jones, M., Fowler, Z., Hughes, B., Mannion, G., Miller, K., Satchewell, C. & Smith, J. (2009) *Improving Learning in College: Rethinking literacies across the curriculum* (London, Routledge).

James, D. & Biesta, G. J. J. (2007) *Improving Learning Cultures in Further Education* (London, Routledge).

Latour, B. (1986) The Powers of Association, in: J. Law (ed.), *Power, Action and Belief: A new sociology of knowledge* (London, Routledge and Kegan Paul).

Latour, B. (1987) *Science in Action* (Cambridge, MA, Harvard University Press).

Latour, B. (1996) *Aramis or the Love of Technology* (Cambridge, MA, Harvard University Press).

Latour, B. (2005) *Reassembling the Social* (Oxford, Oxford University Press).

Law, J. (1994) *Organising Modernity* (Oxford, Basil Blackwell).

Law, J. (2007) Actor Network Theory and Material Semiotics. Version of 25th April 2007, available at http://www.hetrogeneities.net/publications/Law-ANTandMaterialSemiotics.pdf (Accessed 22 February 2008).

Law, J. & Hassard, J. (eds) (1999) *Actor Network Theory and After* (Oxford, Blackwell).

Mol, A. (2002) *The Body Multiple* (Durham, NC, Duke University Press).

Leech, M. (1999) Further education in Scotland post-incorporation, in: T. Bryce & W. Humes (eds), *Scottish Education* (Edinburgh, Edinburgh University Press).

Mulcahy, D. (1998) Designing the User/Using the Design: The shifting relations of a curriculum technology change, *Social Studies of Science*, 28:1, pp. 5–37.

Mulcahy, D. (1999) (Actor-net) Working Bodies and Representations: Tales from a training field, Science, *Technology and Human Values*, 24:1, pp. 80–104.

Nespor, J. (1994) *Knowledge in Motion: Space, time and curriculum in undergraduate physics and management* (London, Falmer Press).

Nespor. J. (2003) Undergraduate Curricula as Networks and Trajectories, in: R. Edwards & R. Usher (eds), *Space, Curriculum and Learning* (Greenwich, IAP).

Roth, W-M. & McGinn, M. (1998) > unDELETE Science Education:/lives/work/voices, *Journal of Research in Science Teaching*, 35:4, pp. 399–421.

Smyth, J., McInerney, P., Hattam, R. & Lawson, M. (1998) Teacher Learning: The way out of the school restructuring miasma, *International Journal of Leadership in Education*, 1/2, pp. 95–109.

Spillane, J. (1999) External Reform Efforts and Teachers' Initiatives to Reconstruct their Practice: The mediating role of teachers' zones of enactment, *Journal of Curriculum Studies*, 31:2, pp. 143–175.

Strathern, M. (1996) Cutting the Network, *The Journal of the Royal Anthropological Institute*, 2:3, pp. 517–535.

Thomson, C. (2003) Further Education in Scotland, in: T. Bryce & W. Humes (eds), *Scottish Education* (Edinburgh, Edinburgh University Press).

Urry, J. (2000) *Sociology Beyond Societies* (London, Routledge).

3

Unruly Practices: What a sociology of translations can offer to educational policy analysis

MARY HAMILTON

1. Introduction and Overview: What's the Story?

First Story: The International Adult Literacy Survey (IALS)

Two researchers arrive at the plate glass and concrete multi-storey office block in central London which houses the Office of National Statistics. There is a security desk at the entrance and they have to sign in to receive their visitor's badge. They are met by one of the survey team who takes them up in the smooth lift to the open plan office where they will be able to peruse the English language version of the test used in the International Adult Literacy Survey (IALS). The IALS is an initiative of the Organization for Economic Cooperation and Development (OECD) an international policy think-tank whose members are the world's richest countries. The IALS has produced an international league table of levels of Adult Literacy in 24 different countries. The researchers sit at a functional table with the test booklets spread out in front of them trying to note down as much as they can. Photocopying is not allowed as the materials are restricted and the power of the test would be lost if they were circulated to unauthorized people. This is a tenet of the psychological testing industry to which the IALS is connected. The security surrounding the test is the first sign of the networks that have produced it and its potential as a powerful actant in the Skills for Life *policy strategy. The researchers will piece together examples of the test from other published research papers and putting these together with their written notes, will publish a critique of the test. This critique will itself become a contributor to the policy process—a weak and minor influence, cited by other researchers but ignored by the dense nodes of the central policy network. The policy process requires that the details of the test remain closed to public scrutiny so that it can play its part as an undisputed rationale for action. Later the researchers will shake their heads as they read the banner headline in the tabloid newspaper which declares: '7 million people cannot read a medicine bottle label'.*

The story of this encounter with the international Adult Literacy Survey is a typical device of ANT analysis (see Moser & Law, 1999; Law, 1999; Callon, 1986). This is not storying for the sake of it or simply to grab attention. It is part of a motivated methodology for attending to the back-room workings of social technologies in the making. The survey is crucial to the policy intervention I will describe in this paper as it is the first move in a gathering actor network that has international origins lying at a great distance

Researching Education Through Actor-Network Theory, First Edition. Edited by Tara Fenwick and Richard Edwards.
Chapters © 2012 The Authors. Book compilation © 2012 Philosophy of Education Society of Australasia.

(both geographically and subjectively) from the further education college classroom where literacy learners gather and a part-time tutor carries out her work.

The world as proposed by ANT is a fluid one and a similar flexibility is claimed by the theorists who use it. The concepts are built and elaborated through application to empirical examples, a conversation between theory and data that is useful for analysing complex social phenomena.

Whilst to date, ANT has mainly been applied to science and technology studies, it is increasingly used to explore innovations in the field of health and in organizational studies (e.g. Vickers & Fox, 2005) There are now some examples of it being used to analyse educational issues (Clarke, 2008; Edwards & Usher, 2007; Fox, 2005, 2009; Kendall & Wickham, 1998; Nespor, 1994, 2006; Verran, 1999; Yasukawa, 2003). Given ANT's interest in the archaeology of innovation, it seems a promising approach to use for tracking and understanding the histories of educational policy reforms which are typically sinuous, layered, conflicted and time-bound.

It also fits with my own area of study, that of literacy studies and a foundational understanding of literacy as part of social practice which sees the meanings and values of literacy to be contingent and situated, shifting according to context, purpose and social relations (Barton & Hamilton, 1998; Barton, Hamilton & Ivanič, 2000). Scholars of literacy studies have described the vernacular, everyday practices of reading and writing. They view institutions as selecting and privileging certain practices (Brandt & Clinton, 2002; Kell, 2006; Leander & Sheehy, 2004; Luke, 2003; Street, 2003). ANT offers a way of understanding how such privileging is achieved. ANT scholars have focused on the social and institutional processes that accompany technological innovations. The same ideas can be applied to educational policies which can be seen as social projects that aim to organize and make tractable diverse everyday lived experience.

This paper takes the philosophical ideas of ANT and applies them to a policy analysis of a recent national educational reform in England, *Skills for Life*. This reform is the latest in a series of policy interventions in an unstable, dispersed and heterogeneous socio-cultural field, that of Adult Literacy education. It is part of a wider reform of post-school education and training that aims to improve its quality and coherence (Finlay *et al.*, 2007; Hodgson *et al.*, 2007; Hamilton & Hillier, 2006). The effort to produce standardised qualifications that will be recognised nationally and internationally, has led to the narrowing of adult participation in education more generally (Tuckett & Aldridge, 2009).

The paper demonstrates what can be gained by way of insight and purchase on this policy initiative by applying the core principles of ANT. Also known as 'a sociology of translations', ANT assumes firstly that social reality is fluid, messy and consists of competing social projects. Secondly, ANT's interest in technological innovation is highly relevant to 21st century social policy making, in which new technologies of governance are being trialled and applied with the aim of imposing order on, controlling, defining and reshaping the disorderly flow of everyday educational practice. Thirdly, through the principle of symmetry ANT asserts that all events and entities (both human and non-human) are potential agents and should be treated in equivalent ways within an analysis; that 'truths' must be subjected to the same process of questioning as 'errors' or deviations, with attention paid to the backroom detail of how policies are made and implemented, things that go wrong as well as 'what works'—a central concern of evidence-based policy. ANT asserts that the effects of power can be traced through assemblies, or mixtures, of objects, animals, people, machines, discourses and so on to which agency is delegated. ANT has always had a particular interest in the role of intelligent machines as hybrid beings that embody human intentions, acting on, amplifying and substituting for their activity.

This is a controversial ontology but one that fits the policy process well, with its heavy reliance on negotiated texts, the discursive power of evidence and the mass media as well as complicated networks of human agents to carry a policy from the stage of formation to implementation. In particular these principles of ANT align with traditions of policy analysis which argue that multiple stakeholders contribute to policy texts and to their implementation and that much practical policy is made through discursive processes (Ball, 1993; Ozga, 2000; Fischer, 2003, 2009). Current policy analysis increasingly recognizes the role of dispersed networks (e.g. Newman, 2001; Hajer & Wagenaar, 2003). This approach has been applied specifically to Adult Literacy policy by Lo Bianco, 2001; and Hamilton & Hillier, 2006.

ANT has evolved a set of conceptual and methodological tools that can be used to excavate the detailed unfolding of social projects like a policy intervention. The individual case I will describe in this paper offers a particularly appropriate context for demonstrating these tools since it follows a concerted effort by a national government to organise a diffuse and informal area of educational practice for the first time. I am especially interested in the role of what Latour (1987, pp. 227 ff) calls 'stable mobiles' in fixing the network effects, since many of the stable mobiles that are created in policy networks are literacy artefacts.

Some approaches to the analysis of policy start by considering constrained and well-defined task-oriented organizations such as individual workplaces or classrooms. Adult Literacy education is not amenable to this approach. It is not characterised by stable or well-bounded shared purposes. Traditionally it has been a field with a shifting membership who do not have clear rights or direct channels of communication for negotiating meaning. At different points in time, it has included numeracy and digital technologies (ICTs) as well as literacy, and English for Speakers of Other Languages (ESOL). It operates across diffuse sites of action—in workplaces, job recruitment and training centres, family and community settings, prisons and Further Education Colleges. As a field of policy and practice it is positioned within complex and competing political agendas including those addressing inequalities, stigma and racism, social inclusion and economic development. In addition, changing technologies destabilise the category of 'literacy' calling into question what counts as reading, writing (Snyder, 1998; Lankshear, 1997; Kress, 2003). This leads to ambivalent engagement and incomplete repertoires of shared resources among participants that leaves many assumptions unarticulated. As Holland and Lave point out, this is not to be critical of the field. These features are often the creative lifeblood of social change and challenge: 'much of what is contested in local struggles is the very meaning of what's going on. The world is not a "given" in this perspective' (Holland *et al.*, 2001b, p. 22). Adult Literacy education is such a loosely-framed field of social action and needs an analytic approach that can deal robustly with issues of power and conflict.

As a philosophical and theoretical approach ANT recognises and validates this picture of the mess, fluidity, contingency and vitality of everyday social practice, and offers resources to explore pathways through it to uncover the workings of power. ANT draws on Foucault's notions of the performative nature of power in micro-interactions and shares his interest in excavating how social projects build and become sedimented and institutionalised within everyday practice. Hence the significance of the opening story of the encounter with the International Adult Literacy Survey.

Using ANT we can develop analytical strategies for dealing with competing policy innovations, unstable or ambiguous social projects and the multiple and shifting perspectives of participants within a given policy initiative. ANT is useful for tracing connections between the local and the global, linking disparate contexts, local action with systemic, without assuming a generic layer of social structure. In this process, actors make what Latour (2005) calls *localising moves* and *globalising connects*, which we will see exemplified later in the stories of the *Skills for Life* policy.

In the following sections I introduce concepts from the theoretical assemblage of ANT to analyse the unfolding of the *Skills for Life* strategy. ANT does not offer a unitary approach to analysis (see Law, 1999) and the concepts discussed here are a selection guided by both the field of policy and practice I analyse (Adult Literacy education) and the discursive methodology that I use. In presenting the analysis, I have followed an accessible format used by John Law (Moser & Law, 1999; Law, 2003) which presents a 'story' followed by an analytic commentary on the processes identified. I have chosen three detailed examples for analysis: the International Adult Literacy Survey (IALS); the Get On! media campaign and the use of Individual Learning Plans (ILPs) by teachers.

A Note on Method

Although the primary interest of this paper is the theoretical contributions of ANT, it is worth pausing on the methodology that has generated the examples I use to illustrate the arguments put forward here.

ANT's preferred methodology is ethnographic and it is especially sympathetic to what Marcus (1995) calls a 'multi-sited ethnography' that links data across different geographical spaces and times rather than focussing on a bounded local context as anthropologists have traditionally done (see also Kaushik, 2009). The choice of significant material to present in an analysis follows the collection of typical ethnographic data (observational records including fieldnotes, interviews with participants, collections of documents and artefacts).

The interpretation of these materials is then guided by the theoretical orientation of ANT following the trajectories of actants (whether people, projects, discourses or objects) and identifying moments in these trajectories where particular moves are made as predicted by the theory. ANT theorists propose a variety of different ways into the data but Callon's four moments (described below) have been widely used in empirical studies. My own choices have been guided by Callon's moments, and also by his idea of 'obligatory passage points' which are pivotal to the creation of an actor network (see Callon, 1986, 1999). I see an OPP as being a node or 'nexus' in the network where there are especially dense connections that can be fruitfully explored to illuminate the work-ings of power and network development. I have also deliberately chosen examples that foreground the agency of non-human actants—a test, a fictional media character and a bureaucratic form.

The stories presented here are, therefore, theoretically motivated choices. They are summaries in my own words, based on oral history and documentary data collected during an ESRC-funded project called *Changing Faces*,[1] as well as my own involvement in the field of Adult Literacy as practitioner, teacher educator and researcher over an extended period of time. Hamilton and Hillier (2006, 2007) present this data in detail analysing the development of Adult Literacy since the 1970s and including extracts from practitioner interviews and documentary evidence.

2. Concepts Useful for Policy Analysis

ANT proposes a number of processes that are involved when a new initiative such as a social policy sets out to organize lived experience. ANT has been called 'a sociology of translations' and the key process I will focus on is that of 'translation' whereby the messy complexities of everyday life are ordered and simplified for the purposes of the project at hand. A major way in which this is achieved is by classifying experience into categories that can be used to monitor and assess both people and programmes. Such categories are useful to official bureaucracies and can be applied across wide populations. Star (Star & Griesemer, 1989; Star, 1999) has worked extensively on classification systems as a key feature of translation with the aim of revealing what she calls the 'ecology of infrastructure'—the naturalized background organization of everyday life that is 'neces-sarily suffused with ethical and political values, modulated by local administrative pro-cedures' (Bowker & Star, 1999, p. 321). Bowker and Star present examples from a wide range of contexts including classifications of diseases, viruses, racial groups and nurses' working practices. In the case of literacy, the powerful processes of selecting and classi-fying determine what counts as real or 'proper literacy' (Lankshear, 1987) privileging certain practices and rendering others invisible or de-valued.

Translation, as Sakari (2006) argues, is not a simple process of making equivalent two different but predetermined entities. It is, rather, a process of articulation—'a poietic social practice that institutes a relation at the site of incommensurability [...] a process of creating continuity in discontinuity' (p. 75). The result is productively emergent, the smoothing of differences, the alignment and sequencing of a number of sub-projects, a set of differences held—precariously—in tension because, as Sakari again points out, 'translation is always complicit with the building, transforming or disrupting of power relations'(p. 72).

In analysing the process of translation ANT researchers are interested in how new mixtures are created; how differences between previously unconnected elements are reconciled. They attend to the features and external links that must be deleted or elided and the continuities that are reinforced through translation. Numerous examples of translation are presented in ANT publications, including the process of scientific inno-vation in an aerospace laboratory (Law, 1994); the efforts of a group of marine biologists to develop an artificial underwater breeding ground for scallops (Callon, 1986); and the introduction of software to coordinate clinical records in a medical context (Bruni, 2004).

Translation is achieved through a number of 'moments' as expressed by Callon. The use of the term moment implies both a freezing of chronological time sequence to hold up an event to close scrutiny and also 'moment' in the sense of a fulcrum of forces around which events turn. This dual meaning is important, because the policy moments I describe here do (like many others) occur in real time as events, but their occurrence is also repeated, simultaneously experienced and performed by multiple actors. As I will show in my examples below, they extend across and are embedded in overlaid time scales (see Lemke, 2000, 2004). The agility of ANT in accepting and enabling such leaps across time and place but also in documenting close up occurrences is part of its unique value.

The first two moments of *problematisation* and *interessement* are hypothetical. The project is untested and exists only as a technical specification (say for production of a new form of renewable energy) or a policy framework and intention that may exist only on paper and in a politician's or activist's dreams. Success in creating an actor network leads to the third and four moments: *enrolment* and *mobilization*. A successful project must be realized through all of these stages.

In reality ANT asserts that it is impossible to ever take translation to a conclusion—there is constant overflow, disentangling from external entities that continue to crowd in and also steal away the actors. Such overflows are ever-present in policy arenas like *Skills for Life*. Let us look at how these moments might map on to the policy reform process.

Problematisation is propositional and hypothetical: it involves defining individual agents that are clearly distinct and dissociated from one another, making these actors indispensable to the action, defining who and what is part of the network and who/what is excluded from it. This is done through framing and deletion: the selection, privileging and categorization of elements (as described by Bowker & Star, 1999) and can often be tracked through discourse moves such as the elision of agency. I would add that problematisation involves imaginative effort—and that policy formation is the creation in the first instance of what Bartlett and Holland (2002) refer to as a 'figured world'. This is a frame of meaning through which the world is interpreted and imagined. A figured world is mediated and materialized through cultural artefacts and can thus lever change in social practices. A good current example of problematisation is the effort of governments to translate the undifferentiated rubbish produced by populations into a project of recycling. This involves creating new categories of waste, new alliances with industries and consumers, and actants such as wheelie bins.

Interessement attempts to impose and stabilize the identity of the other actors defined through the problematisation. This involves interrupting and weakening links between these actors and others that might want to ally with them (a process of deletion that frequently includes what Stephen Ball (1990, p. 18) has called 'a discourse of derision' whereby previous or other possible associations with the problem are referred to as ethically or rationally unsound. A policy initiative must construct a new alliance, collecting the actors together and developing mechanisms for undermining potential competing associations Such mechanisms are defined in and distributed through, for example, the sequence of documents that characterize a new policy and through which, a new 'infrastructure' is imagined which will replace earlier policy regimes and lock the allies into place. This infrastructure creates 'obligatory passage points' where the flows of action and resources come together and through which debates and discourses are squeezed. It is simple to trace the sequence of documents in the case of *Skills for Life*, from the publication of the International Adult Literacy Survey, the Moser review of basic skills, the subsequent policy strategy document and a whole range of implementation guidance. Interessement can be more or less successful in leading to the next moment of enrollment and history is littered with failed policy initiatives that for a variety of reasons were not able to create or stabilize a strong enough network.

Enrolment of agents into networks involves assembling elements and devices, forms of social interactions which will enable the actors to perform the identities required of them within the network. This takes material investments, strong alliances and the skills of policy implementers to make systematic changes feasible. Examples of such devices are the creation of a high-status research centre, production of teaching and learning materials, training courses, accountability measures and so on.

In the final moment of **mobilization** the few come to speak as the many. There is one united voice and a new settlement which is no longer questioned. This is the stage at which 'black boxing' of previously unstable truths and meanings occurs. Policy has succeeded in imposing a new order on a social field—for the time being.

These key concepts of ANT have the potential to be mapped onto elements of social practice and onto key discourse categories such as the uses of metaphor, argument, positioning of social actors, framing, and clision of agency (Fairclough, 2001, 2003; Wodak, 2001). This link with specific features of discourse can be well illustrated through the example of metaphor. When treated as a manifestation of the key process of translation in ANT, metaphor is not just a matter of style or aesthetics, or even a cultural marker, but a fundamental and powerful move in organizing our knowledge of a field. In the example of the recycling project offered above, metaphors of 'gaia' and a shared planet, 'green' versus 'grey' waste, 'global warming' are powerful rhetorical devices designed to organize public knowledge of the environmental impact of individual action and make alliances with scientific evidence and public action. The locus of agency in environmental change—whether human, natural, individual or collective, or unknown—is a pivotal controversy which pulls the emerging network in different directions.

There are some 'big' recurrent metaphors used in discourses of literacy—so big and naturalised that we hardly notice they are fabrications (see Barton, 2007; Bialostok, 2002). They have occurred over a long period of time in UNESCO publications, posters from national literacy campaigns and so on. These metaphors form a powerful cluster that valorises literacy and sets it in a moral framework that affects our view of the people targeted for literacy help. Metaphors of medical disease or a battle against monsters or demons are common (see for example Farkas & Morris, 2003). Another cluster of metaphors see literacy as a set of 'skills' with 'levels' of achievement, people lying at the 'bottom of the heap' and forming an 'underclass'(Welshman, 2006). More specific metaphors refer to the person themselves and their motivation: in current UK policy adults with literacy needs are spoken of as 'socially excluded', 'marginalised', 'hard to reach', or easy targets—the 'low-hanging fruit'. These metaphors have been productively mobilised—and added to—by the *Skills for Life* Policy to problematise and establish a crisis view of literacy as a deficit inherent in individuals.

Finally, as signalled earlier, of special interest to those working in literacy studies is the ANT notion of the creation of 'stable mobiles' with defining rules for their distribution. A network involves a mobilisation of resources or 'agents', which typically includes physical materials, representations and people and the creation of what Latour refers to as 'stable mobiles'. These are representations of aspects of the world that are portable and thus can be accumulated and combined in new ways at a distance, and used to co-ordinate action from within centres of power. Michael Callon explains why stable mobiles are crucial to the assembling of a network: he sees them as stabilising devices that synchronise meanings, and actions across time and space and multiple actors. They are 'boundary objects' that make possible the framing and stabilisation of actions, while simultaneously providing an opening onto other worlds, thus constituting leakage points where overflowing can occur (see Callon, 1999, p. 188; also Law, 1994, p. 24 and Latour, 1987, pp. 227ff).

As discussed in Barton & Hamilton, 2005, the concept of 'stable mobiles' is parallel to ideas of reification and 'textually mediated realities.' thus enabling links to be made with to literacy studies and social cultural theory.

3. The *Skills for Life* Strategy—A Panorama and Three ANT Stories

Having outlined the ways in which ANT might be used in policy analysis, in this section I briefly describe the *Skills for Life* policy strategy and use three detailed examples to develop the analysis. The aim of the analysis is to examine the stabilisation of the social project of *Skills for Life* and to reveal how this is accomplished. As mentioned above, the three examples have been chosen because they can be considered as 'obligatory passage points' where the flows of action and resources of the network come together and through which debates and discourses about literacy are squeezed. More in depth treatment of these examples can be found in Hamilton, 2001, 2009; and Pitt & Hamilton, in preparation.

Panorama

The field of Adult Literacy, Language and Numeracy (ALLN) started in the 1970s with a 'Right To Read' campaign that mobilized many volunteer teachers motivated by the social justice concerns of the time (see Withnall, 1994). A national agency for England and Wales was set up, The Adult Literacy Resources Agency and became a focal point for the new field. During the subsequent 30 years, ALLN moved from the margins of educational policy into the mainstream, gradually gaining in status. This initially unorganised domain of social action has struggled to be recognized as a legitimate area of educational activity having to engage with deep shifts in national policy priorities that redefined the funding sources, goals and discourse of the emerging field.

The *Skills for Life* Strategy is a concerted attempt by the national government of England to shape and organize ALLN for the first time, to establish continuities with school-based literacy education and with the (equally unstable) field of vocational training. Crucially, it has been an attempt to fix the value of literacy for adults—to commodify it. This strategy was one of a number of prominent initiatives supported by the New Labour administration of Tony Blair. It reflected the broader goals of social and educational policy of the time, as well as a characteristic technology of governance that relied strongly on measurement, target setting and micro-managed audit and accountability processes (see Newman, 2001; Hills & Stewart, 2005; Finlay *et al.*, 2007).

Pre-2001, the field of adult basic skills, as it was then known, was a set of 'uncollected' activities, informally monitored. The name, scope and goals of the field were constantly changing. For example, numeracy, ESOL and computer-based learning were sometimes included, and sometimes left out. These ambiguities were acknowledged by all participants—learners, teachers and policy makers (see Hamilton & Hillier, 2006). We can really consider *Skills for Life*, then, as a field that has largely been invented by the New Labour administration.

Building on the National Literacy Strategy in schools and in response to the publication of the OECD's International Adult Literacy Survey findings (OECD, 1997; see also OECD, 2000), a review of Adult Literacy, Language and Numeracy was carried out by Sir Claus Moser in 1999. In 2001, for the first time the national government in England funded a national policy for the field, the *Skills for Life* strategy, setting ambitious targets for improvement (Moser, 1999; DfES, 2001). It created what it self-consciously called an 'infrastructure', designed to rebalance supply and demand in basic skills education and training. The infrastructure consisted of a specialised qualification structure and a set of professional standards for practitioners; core curricula in English for Speakers of Other Languages (ESOL), numeracy, and literacy aligned with performance in school-based subjects; a variety of assessments diagnostic, formative and summative including a national multiple-choice test of Level 2 achievement;[2] planning tools and materials for course providers and a high profile media publicity campaign targeted at specific groups of adults.

In 2004 the strategy met its aim of 750,000 adults gaining an appropriate qualification. Despite controversy about how these targets have been defined and met (Bathmaker, 2007; Sticht, 2003), further targets were set (and have already been achieved) such that by 2010, it is claimed that a total of 2.25 million adults will have improved their basic skills.

After publication of the Leitch Report (Leitch, 2006), *Skills for Life* was reinforced as a successful strategy (see forward to DIUS, 2009) and further targets were projected to 2020. However, following Leitch, the achievement of literacy became conflated with functional skills for employment by embedding literacy in vocational training courses and revising the curriculum with this in mind. The main flow of funding was diverted through employer-led rather than learner responsive provision. Further efforts were made to merge *Skills for Life* qualifications with the key skills qualifications offered in schools, in order to 'tidy up' the field and avoid duplication. However, the very different forms of assessment used for these two previously different fields and client groups have so far proved difficult to reconcile (key skills assessments are much more detailed and comprehensive than the multiple choice test used in *Skills for Life*) A major controversy about funding of ESOL in 2006 removed the entitlement to free courses except for those on welfare benefits. This arose from the over-successful recruitment of ESOL learners and marked the beginning of the marginalisation of ESOL once more from the field of basic skills.

The First Story: The International Adult Literacy Survey—Problematising and Framing

Commentary: The IALS, described in the story at the start of this article, is a crucial early phase of the translation process of assembling *Skills for Life*. It is mainly concerned with problematisation. It offers a rationale for the mobilisation of a network through defining and establishing the existence of a 'problem' to be solved. A set of research findings becomes a bedrock policy rationale. Literacy levels in the adult population (low in relation to other countries) are presented as 'the problem' in relation to desired target levels and the gap in the two becomes the space for policy action. The figure of '7 million adults' becomes a powerful actant in the policy process. We can see this happening very clearly in the translation of IALS to a range of national policy contexts, from the countries of the UK and Ireland, to New Zealand, Sweden and Canada (see for example Veeman *et al.*, 2006, pp. 17–19), all of whom have formulated policies for Adult Literacy and lifelong learning since the results were published. In each country, local actors craft a policy that is tailored to local circumstances but synchronized carefully with international survey measures (including the IALS but often with other surveys too, such as PISA). Over time the IALS findings become a 'black box' of unquestioned assumptions accepted by all as the rationale for moving funding into the literacy area, although how this rationale is then elaborated depends on the wider set of social policy goals espoused by each country. In England, as outlined above, exact targets for Level 2 literacy in the adult population have been set stretching to the year 2020 and a strategy has been devised in relation to these.

The IALS does important work in a previously ill-defined field by fixing the value of Adult Literacy. It deletes the messy local realities of community languages and cultural specifics in literacy practices. It makes a clearly delimited selection among the wide variety of literacy tasks that populations engage with. In so doing, it sets the scene and the parameters for the commodification of Adult Literacy, creating, in Callon's words 'a space of calculability' (see Callon, 1999, p 191) and 'Commodities are here understood as objects, persons, or elements of persons which are placed in a context in which they have exchange value and can be alienated. The alienation of a thing is its dissociation from producers, former, users, or prior context' (Thomas, 1991 p. 39, cited by Callon). Commodification, as mentioned above, was a central aim of *Skills for Life* and great store was put on research claims about how much low levels of literacy cost the economy, and the increase in salary across life that is generated by one level of increase in literacy qualifications.

Value is pinned down through the choice of test items which are circulated around the world and translated into many different languages. It is also pinned down through the invention of levels of attainment, a statistical artefact that enables comparisons among populations to be made and will do even more than the content of the test to shape future provision and policy targets in England.

The breathtaking statistical sleight of hand involved here is apparent to those most familiar with the unruly and intractable field of adult learning where the notion of levels of attainment runs counter to many years of adult learning theory and practice. This is acknowledged in the policy discourse by the metaphor of 'spiky profiles' which is used to acknowledge the uneven attainments of adults whose knowledge actually does not conform to the smooth statistical model underlying the IALS.

However, accepting this figure and the version of reality presented by the IALS becomes an obligatory passage point for all those involved in developing Adult Literacy provision in England. To follow how the IALs contributes to the next moments of translation it is necessary to look at how the survey results are used in the core policy documents of the Moser report (1999) and the *Skills for Life* strategy document itself (DfES, 2001). These documents move the policy rationale into the moment of inter-essement. The identities of the key actants—adult learners, tutors, employers and edu-cational providers—are slotted into place defining how they must see themselves and what they must do as a result (see Pitt & Hamilton, in preparation). The moment of enrolment is also signalled in these documents where corresponding plans for developing an interlocking infrastructure of core curricula, professional standards and a national test—the apparatus of governance—are laid out.

A Second Story: Gremlins—Interessement and—Hopefully—Enrolment

A child's voice calls to her father from another room asking 'Can you help with my homework dad?' 'Go and ask your mother' the father replies from the settee where he is sitting. He is joined on the settee by an ugly grey figure with large pointed ears and a low weaseling voice that taunts him with his difficulties with writing and reading. 'Bad Dad' says the Gremlin, 'Very bad Dad!' This vignette is broadcast at frequent intervals on prime time TV around the country. The content of the advertising is varied to depict different target groups and contexts—for example, home and workplace, women and men. The Gremlins campaign draws on a particular marketing strategy, one used in anti-smoking and other public health campaigns and it is designed to induce people back into adult education courses. The campaign self-consciously aims to counter the stigma and bullying associated with illiteracy (Barnes, 2001) and potential learners are encouraged so see themselves differently, to act in their own best interest and in the interest of the community. The campaign wins prizes. Not only the target audience but other groups are exposed to the campaign: parents, teachers, potential volunteers, children, employers and these groups respond differently, reflecting their particular orientation to the issue of Adult Literacy. Children imitate the Gremlins, people make spoof YouTube videos featuring them, literacy tutors are encouraged to use them in local campaigns, and people dress up as giant gremlins for local photo opportu-nities. Gremlin masks, balloons and stickers promote the message of the ad 'Get Rid of your Gremlins' Some people phone the hotline, some are rebuffed, and some end up on courses. People are encouraged to play with the Gremlin character and even to abuse them. As in all good tie-in advertising campaigns, the Gremlins also feature in a range of merchandise developed to reach inside pubs, offices and sports grounds: the trivia of everyday life—beer mats, post-cards, bookmarks, pencils, scratch cards, desk calendars and paper masks. Advertisements are placed on bus stops and tickets and on the radio and there is a range of more traditional publicity. The beer mats and coasters turn up later as collectibles on E-bay. The first series of the 'Gremlins' advertisements resulted in a large demand for information. By 2009 370,000 people had contacted the helpline (DIUS, 2009, p. 39).

Commentary: The Get On campaign described above is one in a long line of similar mass media campaigns in Adult Literacy, this one more extensive, multi-pronged, with a grand variety of merchandise that is constantly updated. The campaign lasts in various forms across the whole of the period of the *Skills for Life* Policy and illustrates the moments of interessement and enrolment and how these are overlaid in real time. It problematises literacy and invites people to identify in particular ways within the *Skills for Life* framework. It then encourages specific actions such as ringing the hotline or using the Gremlin figures to advertise local provision. It trades in the fears, identities and longstanding metaphors entangled with literacy in complicated was—an extended chain of association that understands literacy as a problem of skills that must be obtained for the good of the community. Over time these have become sedimented in public consciousness as unchallenged assumptions, 'black boxing' the causes and effects of un-met literacy needs.

The mass media campaign and specifically the Gremlins are an attempt by government to create a new actant, a recognized brand that stands in for the discourse of *Skills for Life*, and makes demands on adults with basic skills needs, the tutors and providers who serve them. The aim is to produce material changes in behaviours and promote enrolment. This is only half successful as media campaigns are unpredictable—they are an art not a science—and need constant maintenance work to secure the intended effect. How many people actually use the beer mats and the masks, for example? We asked a carefully structured sample of 78 people from the National Child Development Survey cohort who were interviewed as part of the Changing Faces project to comment on a range of advertising for Adult Literacy, Language and Numeracy since the 1970s, including the Gremlins (Hamilton & Hillier, 2006, pp. 146–7). Though most recognized the Gremlin figures, they were not always clear what the campaign had been about. Even those who did get the message did not see the publicity as targeted at them. From the distantly remembered BBC campaign from the 1970s 'On the Move' to the current Gremlins campaign people felt that Adult Literacy would be good for people who need it, but did not count themselves as being in that group, even though we had chosen them carefully as people whose profiles fitted the current government target group. Several had phoned the helpline on behalf of others. Two had phoned on their own account and one of these had enrolled on a course as a result. The other had been turned away as having problems with spelling that could not be catered for within the local programme. As Sticht (2003) comments, using evidence from the *Skills for Life* survey carried out in 2003 (DfES, 2003): most of the adults targeted by the campaign do not define themselves as in need of basic skills help and have to be persuaded of the role the government has imagined for them—they must, literally, be 'enrolled'.

A Third Story: The Individual Learning Plan (ILP)—Mobilisation and Escape

A group of teachers are gathered for a professional development event in the unfamiliar surroundings of a university campus. They are being asked to reflect on their practices of using ILPs, where the problems lie, what the value and potential of these formative assessment documents are. They exchange stories of forms designed argued over, lost by students, monitored, imposed and sometimes even filled in by administrators. They talk about their 'Level 2 Numeracy' students, about adapting or 'bodging' the forms to make them useable, about how the paperwork sits with the 'real work' of teaching and learning. The conversation strays to observations about their own working conditions, of the situation of part-time teachers, paid by the session and having to squeeze the paperwork into their own time. They return again and again to the idealized point of contact with their students—two heads bent over a form, figuring out the acceptable information to fill in the boxes, two signatures side by side at the bottom denoting agreement, consent, alignment of short medium and long-term goals, SMART[3] targets expressed in the language of the curriculum ('Level 3 Literacy: Speaking, put together a simple sentence'). They report other, sometimes inspiring, sometimes desperate, conversations that occur when the folder is closed—rather like the off-record comments at the end of a research interview. The teachers say they care about the ILP because they care about their students. The ILPs, though technically for, and belonging to, the students are also administrative tools from which information is collected by the colleges and adult educational centres and training bodies and statistics will be generated and used to ensure courses continue to be funded next year. They offer a secure link to curriculum targets, levels of achievement on the national test which are also aligned back to the IALS. ILPs are included in professional development records that follow the student teacher. Through these anchorings the ILP synchronises activity across the network of Skills for Life.

Commentary: The negotiation and use of the ILP illustrates a key moment of mobilization, the consolidation of the network through active involvement of the target actors. The interaction that takes place around the ILP reaffirms the identities of the actants over and over in multiple locations and with many connections to the network. This is possible because the ILP is linked to the core curriculum and to the funding and targets to which the educational providers are tied. In the process of using ILPs teachers perform localising moves (see Latour, 2005) such as using the permissive guidance from central government to produce a version of the ILP that will work in the local circumstances of the college and appropriating it to their own purposes by recording information in ways not intended by policy (as in Burgess, 2008). Simultaneously, they perform globalising connects, the most important of which is to work with their students to translate their individual experience into SMART targets and curriculum elements which will be recognized by funders and inspectors. This aligns their own activities and those of their students with policy goals, and the actions of others involved with *Skills for Life*. These moves are recognized by teachers as problematic and are often accompanied by a sense of discomfort and conflicting demands (Sunderland & Wilkins, 2004; Dennis, 2009).

Policy intention is fixed and delegated through use of the ILP which is a classic example of a stable mobile. It illustrates the crucial point made by Michael Callon that 'it is not the intrinsic competencies of the agent, but that of the equipment and devices which give his/her actions a shape. The importance of the introduction of such tools is starting to be well documented. It is unquestionably one of the essential contributions of science studies' (Callon, 1999, p. 191).

The structure of the ILP—to which teachers actively contribute—'black boxes' the levels and categories of learning—in this case levels and curriculum segments. The IALS sets up the framing process, a core curriculum disperses it within one particular national context; the ILP affirms and continually renews this curriculum at local level. Note, though that this process requires the active participation of both teachers and students which has to be encouraged by the disciplining power of inspection, audit and funding.

4. Conclusions

The aim of this paper has been to demonstrate that ANT can be a productive analytical frame for exploring policy and change in education, a great part of which are accomplished at the discoursal level of social action.

It has shown how institutional activity can impose order on the disorderly flow of social life, creating knowledge that eventually becomes unquestioned truth.

A complex policy reform is choreographed through mobilisation of many actants both human and—as my three examples show—non-human which contain and mandate scripts for action. This endorses Callon's assertion that: '*It is precisely because human action is not only human but also unfolds, is delegated and is formatted in networks with multiple configurations, that the diversity of the action and of the actors is possible*' (Callon, 1999, p. 194) The examples in my analysis also show that even within a strongly framed social project like the *Skills for Life* strategy, things and people constantly escape. Framing is never completely successful; differences held in tension within the 'successful' project sow the seeds of failure and dissolution. Some of these seeds are in the contradictions of the policy itself, some are in the nature of the policy process that renews itself by shifting the spotlight of attention to new arenas.

The differences held in tension include managing specific targets and the broader goals of reducing inequalities between different groups of learners. The goals of lifelong learning and vocational training have to be balanced as do learner-centred and employer/government-led definitions of education; literacy courses as stand-alone or embedded in other, more privileged, subject areas. There are tensions in relationships with employers who are by turn deferred to and obligated to maintain their support for the policy. Finally, the integrity of the different subject areas gathered under the umbrella of *Skills for Life*—ESOL, numeracy, literacy and ICT—has to be managed.

What Escapes from Skills for Life and What Will Remain?

Evidence from a number of reviews and evaluation studies confirms that most of the potential adult learners escape—both because of and in spite of—the relentless pursuit of target numbers. (House of Commons Public Accounts Committee, 2006; Bathmaker, 2007). Many adults in the target groups do not phone the hot-line or enrol on courses. On the other hand, those that do are in the 'wrong' groups. Rather than 'hard to reach' disadvantaged adults, those who come forward are younger, already in fulltime education and training. Or they are ESOL learners who come forward in great numbers and are not welcomed by policy-makers. Despite the high demand for ESOL courses, therefore, ESOL learners escape because of the ambivalence of the government and the general public about how far ESOL learners deserve free educational opportunities (see NIACE, 2006.). Currently ESOL is deleted from *Skills for Life* (in terms of funding and entitlement) but included (in terms of teachers training and curriculum). A footnote in the 2009 *Skills for Life* forward strategy document says ESOL will in the future be 'included in the target as literacy' (DIUS, 2009).

More seriously, in the attempt to reshape the field, Lifelong Learning escapes and finally, the field of Adult Literacy itself loses its identity as a separate field of policy action. The successful alignment of Adult Literacy education with school based 'key skills' and vocational training may result in it disappearing altogether as a recognisable specialism. The government's forward strategy (DIUS, 2009) lays out the future focus on embedding literacy within vocational skills and plans to reinforce the curriculum in line with this. This confirms the direction started by Leitch in 2006 to fully integrate literacy as a vocational skill that will soon be mapped to the national qualifications framework and subsumed by the functional skills of English.

Adult Literacy as a field of educational policy and practice has historically experienced constant transmutation which Skills for Life has fixed and slowed down for while. The chances are that it will stay on the policy agenda of a tenacious Labour administration. DIUS (2009) barely hints at the crumbling state of global markets in 2010 and does not admit any cracks in the façade of *Skills for Life*. It lays out plans to extend the strategy to 2020. However, the policy initiative is already changing shape and a change of government to a Conservative administration could relax the policy hold and see Adult Literacy sink once again down the priority order of skills. Certainly social and educational inequalities will remain and so therefore will the need for adult learning. It is likely that employer interests and the vocational rationale for literacy will continue to be powerful actants.

Evaluating the Theory: Does ANT Live Up to its Promise?

Adult literacy remains an ambiguous social space. Its boundaries are unresolved, with many different social projects and interest groups existing in a variety of relationships to one another, both supporting and competing. In this paper I have argued that given these characteristics, ANT is a particularly promising philosophical and analytic framework to apply to it as it is works with a dynamic view of social life which acknowledges power and contestation and assumes multiple perspectives. Its central metaphor is that of an open field of competing social forces and projects that are continually shifting, with alliances being formed and dissolved. However, like all theories, it invites us to see the world through the selective lens of its own assumptions and metaphors, whilst downplaying its limitations. In the search for better analytical languages for big problems like structure and agency, global and local relations, we need to review and compare theoretical approaches that might work together to develop insights into the social world. Whilst some theories have incompatible ontological and epistemological assumptions, and cannot be combined at will, others do reach toward similar ideas albeit with different emphases and languages of description. As well as literacy studies, compatible theoretical perspectives that I have considered include socio-historical activity theory with its associated ideas of communities of practice and activity systems; Scollon's theory of action mediated by discourse and the notion of a 'nexus of practice' (Scollon, 2001, p. 16) and Bartlett and Holland's (2002) notion of figured worlds, drawing on Bourdieu, Vygotsky and Bahktin. Each of these has features that could helpfully extend the reach of ANT as well as having their own limitations. For example, while ANT has advantages for analysing change and innovation in open systems, activity theory is useful in exploring more bounded and coherent social arenas such as individual workplaces. Both Scollon and Bartlett and Holland develop subtle analyses of subjectivity and meaning making in relation to action—aspects which, as critics have pointed out, are not well addressed within ANT.

ANT's view of social structures as dynamic, not fixed, is a familiar idea in post-modernist thought. However, ANT's approach to agency is more radical and difficult for many people to absorb. According to ANT, agency is not a pre-given individual property of either humans or things but emerges through the relationships that come into being through actor networks. Thus, a powerful actant at one point can be rendered ineffective at another. ANT's insistence that humans and non-humans must be treated, analytically, in the same way with all entities having the potential to exert agency and contribute to the patterning of social life is the point that sceptics of ANT often find hardest to accept. See, for example, Miettinen (1999) who argues that it severs 'agency' from the usual accompaniments of subjectivity, intentionality and identity—all uniquely (we believe) human attributes. My own view is that this is, in fact, one of the most important philosophical contributions of ANT, in that it offers a way for thinking rigorously about agency that frees it from these other qualities. It does not disallow them but neither does it give them a privileged role in the analysis of social projects. There is no attempt to deny the existence of conscious intention: a social project, after all, has to be imagined and recognised by someone.

Although it has not been the purpose of this article, I believe there is a theory of identity that could be teased out of ANT in which identity would be viewed as a network *effect* rather than a cause of action. Like Foucault, identity would be seen as dynamic, dispersed, shaped by social relationships and culturally embedded rather than a quality residing in an individual. ANT might align with identity theorists such as Holland (Holland *et al.*, 2001a) and Butler (1993) who draw attention to the ways in which individuals are positioned by others and by social discourse, cultural artefacts, embodied and material aspects of the world rather than seeing the internal, subjective dimension of identity as a fixed and independent driver of action. Holland's concept of 'figured worlds' proposes that we act in daily life not just in reaction to constraints and forces we encounter, but in relation to imagined realities in which we take on particular identities and act as if they were real. These become 'frames of meaning' through which we interpret social reality and the possibilities for action. In taking on or creating a new 'figured world' we make use of material and cultural artefacts that can be shared in social interactions and which come to have special symbolic significance. Literacy-related artefacts are an important class of these (Bartlett and Holland, 2002). This can be seen in the example of the paperwork record of the ILP described in this article, which grows from selected social facts of an individuals life and both creates and maintains a narrative identity for that individual and those who come into contact with her.

ANT has also been criticized for its a-morality in that it does not pass judgment on the activities of networks nor individual actants except in terms of their effectiveness in increasing the power of the network. I would agree with this. As far as the analytic process goes, ANT challenges the theorist to focus on power relations rather than on moral right or wrong or on the particular perspective of individual beings or categories of being. Unlike critical theory or feminist theory, it does not start from an assumption of unequal distribution of power and resources and set out to rectify this. However, the root impulse of a least some of ANT's major figures (including Law, Latour and Star) is a profoundly democratic one—an interest in dismantling myths about unassailable technological truths and expert wisdom; an even-handed interest in (as Callon puts it) the CEO of a major corporation and the owner of a shell-fish stall; and a belief in the unpredictability and contingency of complex social projects and relationships. I would suggest that ANT's lack of interest in, or disavowal of, fixed social status and hierarchy enables moral and ethical dimensions to be more clearly seen based on its analytic insights. The uncovering of contingency enables activists (not an ANT term!) of whatever persuasion to make practical decisions about where it will be most effective to apply effort within a process in order to shape it.

This stance is valuable to all would be actors (oppressors as well as the oppressed) who have projects to change the world. It aligns with a view, taken by many policy analysts of the unpredictable genesis and trajectory of social policy even when this is promoted in the most rational, scientific and managerial way. When policy is presented as a rational process ANT interprets this as a power play in its own right. ANT aims to uncover the workings of power and to show the instability of social policy thus offering hope for those who would like to take a more activist role in shifting policy in a particular direction.

For me, therefore, ANT opens an ethically and strategically useful perspective on the social world, well worth exploring in the field of Adult literacy policy and in educational research more generally. It is useful, but not definitive. Like the escapees from *Skills for Life*, aspects of the social inevitably escape the social project of ANT.

Notes

1. Changing Faces, a History of Adult Literacy, Numeracy and ESOL 1970–2000, conducted between 2001–2004. Economic and Social Research Council Ref No: R000239387.
2. Level 2 is equivalent to the national test of achievement for 15-year-olds, The General Certificate of School Education, and is also calibrated to the International Adult Literacy Survey.
3. SMART is Specific, Measurable, Achievable, Relevant and Time-bounded.

References

Ball, S. J. (1990) *Politics and Policy Making in Education: explorations in policy sociology* (London, Taylor & Francis).

Ball, S. J. (1993) What is Policy? Texts, trajectories and tool boxes, *Discourse*, 13:2, pp. 10–17.

Barnes, S. (2001) Why Gremlins?, *Update*, 1:12–13 (London, Department for Education and Skills). Available at: http://www.dius.gov.uk/skills/skills_for_life/~/media/publications/S/sflu1 ⟨http://www.dius.gov.uk/skills/skills_for_life/~/media/publications/S/sflu1⟩ (accessed 13 November 2009)

Bartlett, L. & Holland, D. (2002) Theorizing the Space of Literacy Practices, *Ways of Knowing*, 2:1, pp. 10–22.

Barton, D. (2007) *Literacy: An introduction to the ecology of written language*, 2nd edn. (Oxford, Blackwell).

Barton, D. & Hamilton, M. (1998) *Local Literacies: A Study of reading and writing in one community* (London, Routledge).

Barton, D. & Hamilton, M. (2005) Literacy, Reification and the Dynamics of Social Interaction, in: D. Barton & K. Tusting (eds), *Beyond Communities of Practice* (Cambridge, Cambridge University Press).

Barton, D., Hamilton, M. & Ivanič, R. (2000) (eds) *Situated Literacies* (London, Routledge).

Bathmaker, A-M. (2007) The Impact of Skills for Life on Adult Basic Skills in England: How should we interpret trends in participation and achievement?, *International Journal of Lifelong Education*, 26:3, pp. 295–313.

Bialostok, S. (2002) Metaphors for Literacy: A cultural model of white, middle-class parents, *Linguistics and Education*, 13:3, pp. 347–371.

Bowker, G. & Star, S. (1999) *Sorting Things Out: Classification and its consequences* (Cambridge, MA, MIT Press).

Brandt, D. & Clinton, K. (2002) Limits of the Local: Expanding perspectives on literacy as social practice, *Journal of Literacy Research*, 34, pp. 337–356.

Bruni, A. (2004) Shadowing Software and Clinical Records: On the ethnography of non-humans and heterogeneous contexts, *Organization*, 12:3, pp. 357–378.

Burgess, A. (2008) The Literacy Practices of Recording Achievement: How a text mediates between the local and the global, *Journal of Education Policy*, 23:1, pp. 49–62.

Butler, J. (1993) *Bodies that Matter* (London, Routledge).

Callon, M. (1986) Some Elements of a Sociology of Translation: Domestication of the scallops and the fishermen of St Brieuc Bay, in: J. Law (ed.), *Power, Action and Belief. A new sociology of knowledge?* (London, Routledge & Kegan Paul), pp. 196–233.

Callon, M. (1999) ANT—the Market Test, in: J. Law & J. Hassard, *Actor Network Theory and After* (Oxford, Blackwell), pp. 181–195.

Clarke, J. (2008) Assembling 'Skills for Life': Actor-network theory and the new literacy studies in: M. Prinsloo & M. Baynham (eds), *Literacies, Global and Local* (Amsterdam, John Benjamins), ch. 8, pp. 151–170.

Dennis, C. (2009) Controlling the Imagination: How skills for life teachers understand quality. Unpublished PhD thesis, Institute of Education, London.

DfES (2001) *Skills for Life* (London, HMSO).

DfES (2003) *Progress in Skills for Life* (London, HMSO).

Department of Innovation, Universities and Skills [DIUS] (2009) *Skills for Life: Changing lives* (London, HMSO).

Edwards, R. & Usher, R. (2007) *Globalisation and Pedagogy: Space, place and identity*, 2nd edn. (London, Routledge)

Fairclough, N. (2001) The Discourse of New Labour: Critical discourse analysis, in: M. Wetherell, S. Taylor & S. Yates (eds), *Discourse as Data: A guide for analysis* (London, Sage), pp. 229–266.

Fairclough, N. (2003) *Analyzing Discourse: Textual analysis for social research* (London, Routledge).

Farkas, H. & Morris, M. (2003) The Illiterate Man is Like a Blind Man: Soviet posters from the literacy campaign of the 1920s, *Hoover Archives Issue 3*. Available at: http://www.hoover.org/publications/digest/3057746.html

Finlay, I., Edward, S. & Steer, R. (2007) The Impact of Policy on the English Learning Skills Sector, Special Issue of the *Journal of Vocational Education and Training*, 59:2.

Fischer, F. (2003) *Reframing Public Policy: Discursive politics and deliberative practices* (Oxford, Oxford University Press).

Fischer, F. (2009) *Democracy And Expertise: Reorienting Policy Inquiry* (Oxford, Oxford University Press).

Fox, S. (2005) An Actor-network Critique of Community in Higher Education: Implications for networked learning, *Studies in Higher Education*, 30:1, pp. 95–110.

Fox, S. (2009) Contexts of Teaching and Learning: An actor-network view of the classroom, in: Ri. Edwards, G. Biesta & M. Thorpe (eds), *Rethinking Contexts for Learning and Teaching* (London, Routledge).

Hajer, M. & Wagenaar, H. (2003) (ed.) *Deliberative Policy Analysis: Understanding government in the network society* (Cambridge, Cambridge University Press).

Hamilton, M. (2001) Privileged Literacies: Policy, institutional process and the life of the international adult literacy survey, *Language and Education*, 15:2–3, pp. 178–196.

Hamilton, M. (2009) Putting Words in their Mouths: The alignment of identities with system goals through the use of individual learning plans, *British Educational Research Journal*, 35:2, pp. 221–242.

Hamilton, M. & Hillier, Y. (2006) *The Changing Face of Adult Literacy, Language and numeracy 1970–2000, a critical history* (Stoke-on-Trent, Trentham Books).

Hamilton, M. & Hillier, Y. (2007) Deliberative Policy Analysis: Adult literacy assessment and the politics of change, *Journal of Educational Policy*, 22:5, pp. 573–594.

Hills, J. & Stewart, K. (eds) (2005) *A More Equal Society? New labour, poverty, inequality and exclusion (case studies on poverty, place & policy)* (Bristol, Policy Press).

Hodgson, A., Edward, S. & Gregson, M. (2007) Riding the Waves of Policy? The case of basic skills in adult and community learning in England, *Journal of Vocational Education and Training*, 59:2, pp. 213–229.

Holland, D., Lave, J., Aretxaga, B., Gregory, S., Kearney, M., Linger, D. T., Malkki, L. H., Skinner, D., Warren, K. B. & Willis, P. (2001a) *History in Person: Enduring struggles, contentious practice, intimate Identities* (Advanced Seminar Series) (Santa Fe, NM, School of American Research Press).

Holland, D. Lachicotte, W., Skinner, D. & Cain, C. (2001b) *Identity and Agency in Cultural Worlds* (Cambridge, MA, Harvard University Press).

House of Commons Public Accounts Committee (2006) 21st Report of Session 2005–6. Available at: http://www.publications.parliament.uk/pa/cm200506/cmselect/cmpubacc/792/79202.htm (accessed 5 December 2009).

Kaushik, S. R. (2009) Spectres of Marcus: Lively capital, the work of friendship, and 'new' objects of ethnographic interest, in: S. Coleman & P. Von Hellermann (eds), *Multi-sited Ethnography* (London, Routledge Advances in Research Methods).

Kell, C. (2006) Crossing the Margins: Literacy, semiotics and the recontextualisation of meanings, in: K. Pahl & J. Rowsell (eds), *Travel Notes from the New Literacy Studies: Instances of practice* (Clevedon, Multilingual Matters), ch. 7, p. 147.

Kendall, G. & Wickham, G. (1998) *Using Foucault's Methods* (London, Sage).

Kress, G. (2003) *Literacy in the New Media Age* (New York, Routledge).

Lankshear, C. (1987) *Literacy, Schooling and Revolution* (New York, Falmer Press).

Lankshear, C. (1997) *Changing Literacies* (Buckingham, Open University Press).

Latour, B. (2005) *Re-asssembling the Social* (Oxford, Oxford University Press).

Latour (1987) *We Have Never Been Modern* (Brighton, Harvester Press).

Law, J. (1994) *Organizing Modernity* (Oxford, Blackwell).

Law, J. (1999) *Objects, Spaces and Others*. Available at: http://www.lancs.ac.uk/fass/sociology/papers/law-objects-spaces-others.pdf (accessed April 2009).

Law, J. (2003) *Traduction/Trahison: Notes on ANT* (Lancaster, Centre for Science Studies, Lancaster University) Available at: http://www.comp.lancs.ac.uk/sociology/papers/Law-Traduction-Trahison.pdf

Leander, K. & Sheehy, M. (eds) (2004). *Spatializing Literacy Research and Practice* (New York, Peter Lang).

Leitch, S. (2006) *Prosperity for All in the Global Economy: World class skills* (London, HM Treasury).

Lemke, J. (2000) Across the Scales of Time: Artifacts, activities, and meanings in ecosocial systems, *Mind, Culture, and Activity*, 7:4, pp. 273–290.

Lemke, J. (2004) Learning Across Multiple Places and their Chronotopes. Paper presented at the AERA Annual Conference Symposium on Spaces and Boundaries of Learning. Available at: http://www-personal.umich.edu/~jaylemke/papers/aera_2004.htm (accessed April 2009).

Lo Bianco, J. (2001) Policy Literacy, *Language and Education*, 15:2, pp. 212–227.

Luke, A. (2003). Literacy and the Other: A sociological approach to literacy research and policy in multilingual societies, *Reading Research Quarterly*, 38:1, pp. 132–141.

Marcus, G. E. (1995) Ethnography in/of the World System: The emergence of multi-sited ethnography, *Annual Review of Anthropology*, 24, pp. 95–117.

Miettinen, R. (1999) The Riddle of Things. Activity theory and actor network theory as approaches of studying innovations, *Mind, Culture, and Activity*, 6, pp. 170–195.

Moser, C. (1999) *Improving Literacy and Numeracy: A fresh start. The report of the working group chaired by Sir Claus Moser* (London, Department for Education and Employment).

Moser, I. & Law, J. (1999) Good Passages, Bad Passages, in: J. Law & J. Hassard (eds), *Actor Network Theory and After* (Oxford, Blackwell).

Nespor, J. (1994) *Knowledge in Motion: Space, time and curriculum in undergraduate physics and management* (Knowledge, Identity, and School Life Series) (Bristol, PA, Falmer Press/Taylor & Francis).

Nespor, J. (2006) *Technology and the Politics of Instruction* (London, Routledge).

Newman, J. (2001) *Modernising Governance:* New labour, policy and society (London, Sage).

Tuckett, A. & Aldridge, F. (2009) *Narrowing Participation: The NIACE survey on Adult Participation in Learning* (Leicester, NIACE).

National Institute for Adult Continuing Education (2006) *More than a Language. Final report of the NIACE Committee of Inquiry on English for Speakers of other Languages (ESOL)* (Leicester, NIACE).

Organization of Economic Co-operation and Development (1997) *Literacy Skills for the Knowledge Society* (Paris, Statistics Canada and OECD).

Organization of Economic Co-operation and Development (2000) *Literacy in the Information Age: Final Report of the International Adult Literacy Survey* (Paris, Statistics Canada and OECD).

Ozga, J. (2000) *Policy Research in Educational Settings: Contested terrain* (Oxford, Oxford University Press).

Pitt, K. & Hamilton, M. (in preparation) *Challenging Representations: Constructing the adult literacy l earner over 30 years of policy and practice.*

Sakari, N. (2006) Translation, *Theory, Culture and Society*, 23:2–3, pp. 71–86.

Scollon, R. (2001) *Mediated Discourse: The nexus of practice* (London, Routledge).

Snyder, I. (ed.) (1998) *Page to Screen. Taking literacy into the electronic era* (London, Routledge).

Star, S. L. & Griesemer, J. R. (1989) Institutional Ecology, 'Translations,' and Boundary Objects: Amateurs and professionals in Berkeley's Museum of Vertebrate Zoology, 1907–39, *Social Studies of Science*, 19, pp. 387–420.

Star, S. L. (1999) The Ethnography of Infrastructure, *American Behavioral Scientist*, 43, pp. 377–391.

Sticht, T. (2003) *Have the Literacy Skills of Adults in England Improved since 1997? A critique of the Skills for Life Survey of 2003.* Available at: http://www.nzliteracyportal.org.nz/Literacy/United+Kingdom/?url_startrow=20&url_expand=728 (accessed 27 April 2009).

Street, B. (2003) What's 'New' in New Literacy Studies? Critical approaches to literacy in theory and practice, *Current Issues in Comparative Education*, 5:2, pp. 1–14.

Sunderland, H. & Wilkins, M. (2004) ILPs in ESOL: Theory, research and practice, *REFLECT*, 1, pp. 8–9.

Thomas, N. (1991) *Entangled Objects, Exchange, material culture and colonialism in the Pacific* (Cambridge, MA, Harvard University Press).

Veeman, N. Ward, A. & Walker, K. (2006) *Valuing Literacy: Rhetoric or reality?* (Calgary, Detselig Enterprises).

Verran, H. (1999) Staying True to the Laughter in Nigerian Classrooms, in: J. Law & J. Hassard, *Actor Network Theory and After* (Oxford, Blackwell).

Vickers, D. & Fox, S. (2005) Powers in a Factory, in: B. Czarniawska & T. Hernes (eds), *Actor-Network Theory and Organizing* (Frederiksberg, Copenhagen Business School Press).

Welshman, J. (2006) *Underclass: A history of the excluded 1880–2000* (London, Continuum Books).

Withnall, A. (1994) Literacy on the Agenda: The origins of the adult literacy campaign in the United Kingdom, *Studies in the Education of Adults*, 26:1, pp. 67–85.

Wodak, R. (2001) The Discourse-historical Approach, in: R. Wodak & M. Meyer (eds), *Methods of Critical Discourse Analysis* (London, Sage), pp.63–95.

Yasukawa K. (2003) Towards Social Studies of Mathematics: Numeracy and actor-network theory, in: S. Kelly, B. Johnston & K. Yasukawa (eds), *The Adult Numeracy Handbook: Reframing adult numeracy in Australia* (Sydney, NSWALNARC and Language Australia), pp. 99–107.

4
ANT on the PISA Trail: Following the statistical pursuit of certainty

RADHIKA GORUR

In this era of uncertainty, education policy makers appear to rely increasingly on scientific evidence to provide certainties, both for policy direction and policy evaluation. In 2009, 68 countries, representing over 90 percent of the world's GDP, participated in the fourth PISA survey. The words of Australia's then Federal Minister for Education, Julia Gillard, illustrate the reliance on evidence:

> ... good evidence is the key to giving us the pre-schools, schools, training organisations and universities we need ... For over a decade, debates about knowledge and skills in Australia have been based on *the opposite of evidence—prejudice* ... . The Rudd Labor Government was elected with a mandate to end that approach, with a new emphasis on evidence-based reform. (The Hon Julia Gillard, Federal Minister for Education, 2008a, my emphasis)

Whilst governments can collect national performance data, studies such as PISA provide the reference points that make international comparisons possible. PISA data is produced specifically to aid policy making through the establishment of apparently universal standards and indicators against which systems and schools can be evaluated. Surveys such as PISA are not only used to justify decisions (Steiner-Khamsi, 2006), they appear to suggest—perhaps even determine—policy direction:

> [W]e test our students against students from around the world in international tests—they're called PISA. And the message from those tests has been that we aren't extending our highest-achieving students as well as we should and this nation has what is referred to by the statisticians as 'a long tail of students who don't meet minimum benchmarks' ... Well, we're determined to change that ... (Gillard, 2008b)

Viewed as the opposite of prejudice, and capable of giving 'messages' to policy makers, PISA appears to have become a modern day Delphic Oracle which governments consult to get policy direction. Appearing unbiased and neutral, it speaks in a detached manner in terms of 'facts and figures', giving policy makers information about their own countries from its lofty vantage point. To what extent is this reliance on PISA—this *faith* in

Researching Education Through Actor-Network Theory, First Edition. Edited by Tara Fenwick and Richard Edwards.
Chapters © 2012 The Authors. Book compilation © 2012 Philosophy of Education Society of Australasia.

PISA—justified? How does PISA acquire this Apollonic voice to speak about the world's education systems? What is the nature of this knowledge, and how is it produced? Should policy makers consult this PISA-Pythia for policy 'messages'? It is these questions that I address in this paper, using some of the resources provided by actor-network theory (ANT).

ANT and the 'PISA Laboratory'

There is no single unified theory called 'actor-network theory', but some central concepts in this 'disparate family of material-semiotic tools' (Law, 2007) can be identified. ANT holds that ideas, practices and 'facts' are effects of heterogeneous webs of relations between actors, or 'assemblages', a notion similar to Deleuze's 'agencement' (Law, 2008). This anti-foundationalist stance is in keeping with Foucault's poststructuralism; but while Foucault drew attention to the relational production of epochal epistemes, ANT directs its attention more locally to particular actor-networks (Law, 2007).

ANT offers a way to understand how ideas come to be established, be they the usefulness of a machine, the veracity of a scientific fact, or the desirability of a policy directive. Using the notion of *translation*, relations between entities that make up the assemblage are traced. The focus is on the active process of *assembling*, and on how realities are *performed* into being. And in this assemblage, the actants are heterogeneous, including both humans and non-humans.

With a commitment to relationality, ANT regards distinctions and divisions as effects rather than essential qualities, and does away with *a priori* dualisms such as human and non-human, social and technical, and macro and micro. In this study, we will find that the same uncertainties, the same anxieties, the same arguments, with which policy makers are engaged outside, in 'society', are replicated inside the 'PISA laboratory'; the division between 'science' and 'politics' is an achievement.

Early ANT studies such as Latour and Woolgar's *Laboratory Life: the social construction of scientific facts*, Michael Lynch's *Art and Artifact in Laboratory Science* and Latour's *Science in Action* and *Pandora's Hope* dissolved the division between a representational and neutral 'science' on the one hand and a messy, prejudiced, controversial 'politics' on the other (Barry, 2009). Exploring laboratories as ethnographers would an exotic culture, they made visible the practices by which human and non-human entities are imbricated in the production of scientific facts.

In this study, we will enter the 'PISA laboratory', and observe how PISA scientists classify and order the outside world into definable categories, collect samples from the field, use other established sciences such as mathematical modelling, and employ socio-material inscription devices that help to order and preserve data in particular ways. Once all the samples are gathered and detached and prepared for processing, the PISA offices become a *centre of calculation*, where the data can be combined in different ways to produce PISA facts. As the story of PISA unfolds, we see the hesitations and the provisionality of its knowledge gradually coalescing into 'facts'. What is produced as 'PISA knowledge' depends on its particular practices, such as the choice of certain subjects or the use of certain statistical techniques.

The argument made here is for a suspension of the division between a rational and representational 'science' on the one hand, and a messy and irrational 'politics' on the other. To view scientific evidence as an assemblage, a reality performed into being, rather than a representation of a pre-existing truth, is to convert PISA knowledge from a 'matter of fact', something that is beyond dispute, into a 'matter of concern,' something that is available again for discussion (Latour, 2004). Given the reliance of PISA and its influence on education policy across the world, to perform such an analysis is to engage in a 'politics of fact' (Potter, 2008, p. 174). To recognise the performativity of PISA is to make it possible to *interfere* in the relations that produce these facts, and in the realities being produced (Law, 2008).

Although the story I tell here is one of how 'PISA' is assembled, multiple PISAs are being performed. To generalise crudely for the purposes of illustration, psychometricians perform a PISA of statistical sophistry within the limitations of large-scale testing, commensuration and standardisation; subject experts, a PISA of pedagogic innovation, honouring application of knowledge over curriculum; country representatives, a PISA of patriotic advantage, as though a high PISA score is in itself an advantage to the country, rather than an indicator of possible future advantage, and the OECD, an admonishing PISA of standards, policy imperatives, efficiencies and aspirations. The point is not simply that a singular PISA is viewed differently from different standpoints, but that PISA is ontologically variable and multiple PISAs are being performed into being (Law, 2008). This understanding of ontological variability is central to ANT, particularly in more recent ANT accounts. Yet I choose to tell this story with the more old-fashioned approach of a laboratory study, because the politics I want to perform here is more concerned with epistemology than ontology. My aim is to interrupt the view of scientific evidence as neutral and representational, and to dissolve the divide between science and politics as well as reality and fabrication. Laboratory studies suit this purpose admirably.

'Classic ANT' studies have been criticised on the grounds that they unwittingly reify the very essentialisms they seek to interrupt. As ANT studies trace the trajectory of their objects of study from disorder to order, the result is shown as an achievement by consensus, rather than something that is (or can be) contested (Berg & Timmermans, 2000, p. 33). But in this study, rather than highlight how PISA has successfully become accepted, I focus on its fragility and argue for an opening up and a questioning. Rather than an aloof, scientific, all-knowing disembodied voice, an Oracle on a hill with the power to advise and foretell, PISA becomes de-mystified, squarely situated in the same messiness as the 'social' world outside the laboratory, open, again, to intervention.

Such an understanding makes politicians not only of the researchers in the PISA laboratory, but also this researcher, writing this paper. The writing and publication processes involve the same negotiations and arguments, the same orderings and constraints, the same testing of what the 'collective' can swallow (Latour, 1999, p. 19), as laboratory practices. I make no claim to be 'a voice from nowhere', observing PISA from a detached bubble. This assemblage is as much imbricated in messiness and politics as it is in research work. Readers are thus invited to question and intervene in this account, just as they are invited to engage with PISA's account of the world's education systems.

PISA: An Overview

PISA was developed in the late 1990s by the OECD in response to a growing demand from member countries for reliable educational output data to supplement their extensive input data.[1] Conducted every three years, the PISA survey has two components: the instruments that measure 15-year-olds in the areas of reading, mathematical and scientific literacy;[2] and those that collect a wide range of data about factors that are thought to be associated with education, such as student motivation, family economic status and certain school factors. PISA must find ways to standardise and measure these diverse bits of information and make them commensurate so that we may talk about children in Peru and school systems in Belgium and teacher salaries in Australia in one breath, as though it were the most natural thing in the world.

Although PISA surveys are developed and managed by an independent consortium[3] on contract to the OECD, PISA itself is a collaborative effort involving member countries at almost every step of the complex process of data gathering and analysis. Only OECD member country representatives participate in the construction of the test. Each participating country is responsible for adhering to strict PISA guidelines on sampling, collecting, storing and coding data. The tests are marked and the results collated and analysed, and then disseminated to the participating countries. The 'OECD average' becomes the standard against which countries can rate how they measure up. Interested countries prepare their own country reports based on the data and analysis. PISA results are published in a variety of OECD documents and reports, most notably in its annual publication, *Education at a Glance*.

OECD's Growing Confidence in International Indicators

The OECD engaged seriously in developing comparative indicators for member nations around 1987.[4] In the early stages, a number of difficulties were highlighted. The classification of concepts was extremely challenging. Comparing even seemingly simple indicators such as enrolment figures was complicated by 'the heterogeneity of definitions', and there were challenges in 'moving from broad statements of agreed concerns and values to operational definitions of specific indicators' (Bottani & Walberg, 1992, pp. 11, 12). 'Speculative' fields such as 'processes, attitudes and expectations', and the reluctance of some countries to reveal certain information caused difficulties. Given this, claims made about what the indicators could achieve were modest and cautious. Consistent measurement was seen as enabling identification of trends over time and informing policy decisions, but establishing causality was considered problematic:

> Indicators cannot provide a precise interpretation of past events, offer clear judgements about present conditions, or point to specific policy remedies for problems that are identified. However, they can generate important new understandings about how education systems are functioning. (Bottani & Walberg, 1992, p. 10)

Over time, the OECD has gained much confidence in the usefulness of these indicators:

[T]his analysis can compare the degree of association with educational outcomes of various factors in different countries. At the individual level, such factors include socio-economic background, immigration status and cultural possessions in the home. At the school level, they include student perceptions of instructional practices, disciplinary environment and, importantly, the collective socio-economic background of students at each school. At the school system level, the extent of school autonomy and the structural organisation of students in secondary education can be compared to the overall performance and distribution of the performance of students aged 15. (OECD, 2007b, p. 9)

The old hesitations and caveats are replaced by a new assuredness in its ability to inform and guide policy makers.

Critiques of PISA

As PISA's influence has grown, so has criticism of the program. Technical criticisms concern themselves with methodological issues and the validity of findings. PISA's One Dimensional Item Response Theory is criticised for reducing the analysis of responses to a single dimension (Bracey, 2008). Bautier and Rayou show that students' responses on PISA tests can be correct or incorrect for reasons that cannot be envisioned through an *a priori* analysis of items (2007). Translations to different languages have also been problematic in some instances. Test items have been criticised as being verbose and of unfamiliar style for many students.[5]

Sociological and political criticisms have focused on the preoccupation with PISA rankings and with accountability and standardisation in general. Simola (2005) believes comparative data have become an 'international spectacle' and a process of 'mutual accountability', raising political and epistemological questions alongside methodological ones. In the same vein, Corbett (2008) finds the quest for 'edumometers' such as PISA to be another manifestation of neoliberal commodification. Others are concerned that repeated constructions and reconstructions of statistical interpretations could reinforce regional stereotypes (Stack, 2006). The dangers of classifying and labelling groups have been highlighted (Connolly, 2006). The deployment of PISA and its role in shaping and legitimising policy, and in creating spaces of convergence and difference, particularly in Europe, have also been highlighted by Grek and others (Grek, 2007; Grek, Lawn & Ozga, 2009).

Realists who believe in facts as representations of reality offer technical criticism, on the assumption that better techniques will present a truer picture of reality. Constructivists who believe that facts are fabrications produced by scientists deconstruct and debunk. I adopt a Latourian stance here and discard the premise that 'reality' and 'fabrication' are opposites. My critique concerns the more fundamental issue of how PISA knowledge, indeed, *any* knowledge, is produced and how it establishes its apparent universality. I am not interesting myself in the politics surrounding the development of tests such as PISA; instead, I focus on the philosophical question of scientific reference through an empirical study of the production of PISA knowledge, using the theoretical resources of actor-network theory.

Background to the Study

This paper arises from a larger, on-going study of evidence-based policy making, using the role of PISA in Australian education policy as an illustrative case. That study is based on ministerial media releases, OECD and Australian government policy documents and reports, and 18 in-depth interviews with high-ranking former OECD officials; former and current PISA officials and Australian education bureaucrats; and several policy advisors. It seeks to understand the multiple assumptions and orderings in the worlds of 'evidence making' and 'policy making' in education today.

As this was a doctoral research study with a curiosity about evidence-based policy making, and the interviewees were all very senior and high-ranking individuals, most with PhDs, the semi-structured interviews took on the air of joint explorations of a complex and interesting phenomenon, to which interviewees generously contributed with their very rich and diverse experiences.

This paper relies mostly on the accounts provided by two interviewees. One is a very high-ranking PISA official who has been involved with PISA from its inception in a very senior capacity. The other, a former PISA employee, has conducted many analyses of data arising from PISA and other international comparative studies. In addition, OECD documents and a book on psychometric assessment have also been used.

In many ways, this study follows in the footsteps of Latour's study of the Amazonian rainforest in *Pandora's Hope* (Latour, 1999) where he traced the practices of scientists as they sought to establish a fact. Latour's question was: 'how do we pack the world into words?' (p. 24). What is the relationship between nature and language?

Like the rainforest of Boa Vista, the unmanageable terrain of 68 countries has to be made manageable through mapping. Spokespersons have to be found to speak for millions of 15-year-olds. A few questions have to stand for the hopes of countries' futures. Data have to be made transportable and combinable in different ways. Incommensurate entities have to be made commensurate and newly sensible within a single spatio-temporal frame.

Making PISA Knowledge

Managing Complexity

The first critical issue in measurement is deciding what to measure. Out of a vast array of possibilities, the PISA Governing Board must decide which aspects of learning can inform:

> ... how well students, at age 15, are prepared to meet the challenges they may encounter in future life ... [and] ... the ability of students to continue learning throughout their lives by applying what they learn in school to non-school environments, evaluating their choices and making decisions. (OECD, 2006, p.7)

Retrospectively, this sounds straightforward and uncontroversial. But settling on what to assess was rife with debate and contestation.

> Early on the challenges were bringing everyone together, to do something that was acceptable to all of them and in part captured their vision but wasn't trivial. What I mean by that is, it is about developing what it is that you will test. What it is you will value in the assessment ... . So I thought the challenge was to be somewhat more forward looking and innovative and try and take some risks and test what everyone thinks they want, what they do see as important, regardless of whether it is in the curriculum or not. (Senior PISA official)

From the outset, then, PISA has been about values as much as 'facts', politics as much as 'Science'. OECD member countries display great diversity in values, priorities and practices in their education systems. The debates attempt to ensure that the investment in PISA pays off in terms of information that is useful to their country.

The arguments are settled at last, and the decisions are inscribed and held in place with signatures. Ironically the appropriateness of the decision will only become apparent in the future, when countries' PISA scores and their eventual prosperity can be correlated. For now, PISA has to build this edifice of evidence on faith—on uncertain foundations and assumptions, based on agreed policy priorities of the member countries.

> I guess we need to see in 10 years' time if Finland[6] is doing the best—we can't validate that [yet]. (Senior PISA Official)

Once this emphasis on preparation for the future was agreed upon, the domains to be tested had to be identified. PISA settled for reading, mathematical and scientific literacy—but not entirely because they are the most valued skills.

> Reading, science and maths are there largely because we can do it. We can build a common set of things that are valued across the countries and we have the technology for assessing them. So there are other things like problem-solving or civics and citizenship—that kind of thing where there would just be so much more difficulty in developing agreement about what should be assessed. And then there are other things like team work and things like that. I just don't know how you'd assess them in any kind of standardised way ... . So you are reduced to things that **can** be assessed. They've tried writing—but ... the cross-cultural language effect seems too big to be comparable. So the things we assess are a combination of the things we value and the things we can do—I think it sends an odd message about science, perhaps, but I don't think anyone would argue about literacy and numeracy. (Senior PISA official)

By default then, the 'skills for the 21st century' are simply those that are currently assessable on a large scale. As Skillbeck (2006) points out, there is little said about such issues as 'values, creativity, and emotional development'. For now, these skills will serve as representatives of others that are currently too difficult to assess. Debates about what to test are settled in this very pragmatic problem of standardised assessment.

But what, within each domain, is important? How are the concept of 'literacy' and the idea of 'application' to be translated into test items? Developing the test within each domain was the responsibility of the Functional Expert Group (FEG), a small group of four or five members with a Chair. The FEG set the framework and the parameters for the kinds of questions that were suitable. The frameworks acted as filters, socio-material technologies that sorted the relevant factors from the non-relevant ones. The FEG needed to ensure that an adequate and fair number of questions relating to different skills and concepts deemed important appeared in the test, and this required expert judgement. This framework and its categories were set up *before* the test items could be developed. A Cartesian grid, with its cells neatly arrayed in rows and columns, it lay waiting like so many prison cells, ready for the task of imposing order on the chaotic debates that were soon to ensue.

> For example—if we take mathematics, mathematics is so broad. To pin it down and say 'Mathematics consists of ...' [is very difficult to do]. What will we focus on? ... And very often it depends on who the chair is, often he brings along his own ideas. (Former PISA official)

The FEGs had many constraints to deal with. The time allocated to the minor domains was quite small and this severely curtailed the number of questions that could be asked. In large-scale assessments, the greater the number of questions in each concept, the greater the confidence one can have in the data. This forced a choice between a few questions over a larger set of concepts, or more questions within a narrow band of concepts.

After the FEG framework was set up, contributions were invited from every participating country.[7] However, most of the contributions did not fit the framework.

> [T]he specific direction of the PISA framework is about application of mathematics, where mostly, in schools, the focus is the curriculum ... Actually finding very good application items in mathematics is very difficult, as it turns out. (Former PISA official)

When they *did* find questions that would fit the framework, another problem was encountered: some questions just did not translate easily into other languages. Moreover, there were arguments about cultural bias and the possible disadvantage posed by questions. Even as the frameworks struggled to ensure order and structure, people befuddled and obfuscated issues. Even as science attempted to impose control, politics kept cropping up and delaying matters. The most vexatious part of PISA was getting agreement on the choice of test items.

> Mostly people quarrelled about the obvious things—you can't test this because this is not in our curriculum—people seem to lose sight of the underlying principles and issues and things you are trying to assess, and be blinded by the superficial content. (Senior PISA Official)

However irritating these discussions might have been, it was important to allow everyone to be heard, and for the process not only to *be* fair, but to be *seen* to be fair.

> [W]e can get very heated arguments about whether or not some items should be included, because [the country representatives] feel there is a bias against certain countries. So there are review meetings and forums for discussing this,

and every country can send their experts there. But it will be unmanageable if the group becomes very large. So in the end, the Expert Group may make a decision having collected ideas from everyone. So at least the processes are made to be seen as being fair, by giving everyone the opportunity to express their opinion. (Former PISA Official)

Although the representatives are there to voice and canvass opinions, it is empirical evidence that ultimately counts. Potential items are field tested in every country for bias.

People will usually say a lot of things because they want to be protective about their countries and very often the things that people say have no basis ... So we don't only judge the bias by what people say, there is always a field trial in every country so we have statistical evidence about whether those items are biased or not. (Former PISA Official)

The framework, the field testing, the careful selection of questions—all ensure that the few items that are selected are worthy representatives of others. At every point there is a translation—from 'knowledge and skills for life' to 'literacy, numeracy and scientific literacy', to a few items that stand for these literacies. The few test items, validated by the framework and the field testing, refer to the three literacies being tested, which in turn represent the knowledge and skills for life, which in turn represent the work of millions of teachers in tens of thousands of schools in a sizeable portion of the world, and stand for the performance of education systems. Having gained a selection of acceptable test items, we are finally able to move to the next stage, where we encounter fewer argumentative humans, and more objects and socio-material devices such as mathematical models. These devices, themselves presumably once controversial, are now able to quell controversy.

Cutting the Ties That Bind

As important as it is to choose the right questions, the actual test items are themselves irrelevant; as long as the identified variable is being tested, the exact test items are irrelevant. Thus confidence in measurement is at once dependent on the careful choice of test items, and also independent of the exact items chosen. Similarly, for a test to be dependable, it should not matter who administers or scores the test. Biases are minimised by putting in place certain measures:

To ensure objectivity[8] of measures based on judgements, it is usual to provide judges with clear guidelines and training, to provide examples to illustrate rating points (e.g., samples of student writing or video tapes of dance performances), to use multiple judges, procedures for identifying and dealing with discrepancies, and statistical adjustments for systematic differences in judge harshness/leniency (Masters, 2001, p. 11).

Inscriptions act as *prescriptions*, acting even *before* the judges have begun their work, mediating their harshness/leniency and standardising their judgements.

The relationships between the student, the teacher and the learning are *uncoupled* from each other. The teacher and the test have already become 'floating' entities, replaceable by other assessors, questions and test items. And as we will see shortly, this is soon to become the fate of students as well. It is this independence that allows entities to become standardised and commensurate.

Gaining Mobility

For a test to usefully measure ability, it must contain items of varying levels of difficulty, graduated at incremental levels that are evenly spaced. This *interval property* is of great significance. Once a test has acquired interval property, a person's ability can be calculated (or, rather, the *probable ability can be predicted*) on the basis of responses to a few test items. One model that allows such calculations is the Rasch model, in which ability and the difficulty level are marked at equal intervals and measured in units called *logits* (Masters, 2001). The interval properties of both the difficulty levels and ability levels allow for relative abilities of students to be expressed as ratios which are constant. This means that comparison between students is possible *irrespective of the level of difficulty of the tasks they have attempted.*

> When data fit the Rasch model, it is possible to compare abilities without knowing, or even having to estimate, the difficulties of tasks. This is a unique feature of the Rasch model. (Masters, 2001, p. 23)

As test items lose context and particularity, they gain standardisation. Interval property at once standardises both test items and student performance, and not only allows calculations to be made on items students have answered, but also predict their performance on items they have not. Thus a student's ability can be judged on the basis of questions never even presented to the student.

To pass the Rasch test, data must 'fit' the expectations of the mathematical model. Any data which appears anomalous is seen as evidence of some irregularity or error. Just as the frameworks dictated which test items were admissible, the Rasch model determines which performances are acceptable. The validity of the test items and the validity of the model are thus mutually performed by socio-material ordering devices.

PISA test items are field tested nationally to determine their suitability for inclusion in the test. For a test to be valid, the level of difficulty of test items needs to be *stable* across populations.

> [A]n item may be deleted from PISA altogether if it has poor psychometric characteristics in more than ten countries (a *dodgy item*); it may be regarded as not-administered in particular countries if it has poor psychometric characteristics in those countries but functions well in the vast majority of others. (OECD, 2009, p. 146)

The limit of 10 countries is arbitrarily[9] decided as the threshold of tolerance[10] for dodginess. Carefully calibrated, and free from any 'dodgy items', we now have a bank of stable items which can be used with confidence to gather information about students' ability as precisely as possible, and with as little bias as possible.

All the elements are now detached, measurable and mobile. The teachers, the test items and the students have bowed out, no longer relevant in their particular forms. The bustle of the classroom and the fuss of real people and things have been translated into a neat, two-dimensional, ordered world of logits. And because logits are standard for a given pool of test items (Wright & Stone, 1979), data from PISA tests can be compared across time and place. The various bits of data can be worked on, manipulated and combined in new and different ways to create new patterns and understandings.

Tying Things Together

Even as the processes of reduction and detachment are taking place, a simultaneous process of amplification is also occurring. The translated entities are able to stand for and speak on behalf of larger groups, and new and different associations are made possible. Standardisation enables generalisability and comparison.

The greater the numbers of test items and students tested, the greater the reliability of the test. But testing is expensive and time-consuming. To make testing feasible and efficient, a sampling process is undertaken so that a few students' performance will represent the performance of the nation. And using the principles of Item Response Theory (IRT) the number of items on which students will be tested is increased.

> [Y]ou don't need to ask every child the same set of questions ... If you go to a more complicated technique like IRT, there are ways of putting kids' scores on to a common metric that allows them to be tested on different testing materials. So rather than having one two-hour test we have 13 two-hour tests.[11] And that gives us greater coverage of the content domain. (Senior PISA Official)

Several students together make up one test-taker, a single test is distributed among many test-takers. It is by this curious intermingling of mathematics, humans, negotiated representatives of knowledge and pragmatic issues of time and money that PISA knowledge gradually emerges.

To compare 15-year-olds' performance in three domains on a common test across much of the world is astonishing, but perhaps not all that useful for policy-making. Many questions remain; for instance, what is the correlation between socio-economic status (SES) and performance? Does gender play a part? Do the type of school, or practices such as streaming, influence performance? What attitudes do students have towards learning certain subjects, and how does this influence their performance?

To produce answers to these, more data needs to be gathered. This is done using a 30-minute 'background questionnaire' for students, and a 20-minute questionnaire for school principals. But these questionnaires about home background, approaches to learning and perceptions of learning environments have no backing from known science. There is no guarantee that the questions that are asked on the questionnaires, even if answered accurately, serve as indicators of the attribute being measured. For example, early on, PISA was interested in the link between parent involvement in students' schoolwork, and students' performance. The assumption was that when parents took an interest in children's school experience and schoolwork, performance would be better. But:

That didn't work because if your parents are asking you a lot about your schoolwork, guess what the problem is—you are not a good performer, right? ... So that didn't get used ... The cultural capital—whether you own a violin or a piano or go to concerts and stuff—that didn't get used—but the possessions did get used. And the books in the home is always there—it is very odd, I haven't understood why books in the home is such an important thing, it is obviously some kind of indicator of the environment that fosters an interest in education, but we have never actually unpacked what it is about the books in the home. (Senior PISA Official)

Moreover, 15-year-olds are often inaccurate in reporting about parental income, education levels or professional status. Mathematics again comes to the rescue in dealing with erratic teenagers. Raw responses are converted to ranges, and thus converted, the answer is often within the range in which it belongs.[12]

But PISA has access to yet more resources. For years, the OECD has been collecting information on:

Indicators describing the general structure of the education systems (their demographic and economic contexts—for example, costs, enrolments, school and teacher characteristics, and some classroom processes) and their effect on labour market outcomes are already routinely developed and applied by the OECD. (OECD, 2006, p. 15)

This information too can now be combined with the new data collected to create new knowledge about school systems around the world.

Becoming a Centre of Calculation

What PISA has achieved with these moves is the ability to 'act at a distance' by 'mobilising the world' (Latour, 1987, p. 223). Students in distant lands, school systems across oceans and deserts, have now been 'brought home' by following these steps:

(a) render them *mobile* so that they can be brought back; (b) keep them stable so that they can be moved back and forth without additional distortion, corruption or decay, and (c) ... combinable so that whatever stuff they are made of, they can be cumulated, aggregated, or shuffled like a pack of cards. (Latour, 1987, p. 223)

An enormous variety of things have now been converted into inscriptions on a completed form, coded according to pre-designated structures, and brought safely to the PISA offices. The students and their learning—indeed, whole school systems, represented by these students, have all been 'detached, separated, preserved, classified, and tagged' (Latour, 1999, p. 39). The world has now been transformed into 'two-dimensional, superposable, combinable inscriptions' (p. 29), so that scientists are able to sit in the comfort of their offices and reassemble, reunite and redistribute them 'according to entirely new principles *that depend on the researcher, on the discipline ... and according to the institution that shelters them*' (ibid, my emphasis). Speaking of PISA analyses, Skillbeck says:

> The authors have done a remarkable job in tabulating and modelling data; in constructing a mass of highly informative tables and figures, which condense and interrelate data in most intricate ways; establishing patterns, through text and visual representation, between pre-school attendance and later mathematical performance, school admittance policies (social intake), and school policies and practices; and in assessing the impact of school resources and teacher-pupil relations on performance. (Skillbeck, 2006, p. 100)

What these entities lose in becoming detached from their contexts, they gain in becoming commensurate and combinable. The world's educational systems 'become a chart, the chart ... becomes a concept, and the concept becomes an institution' (Latour, 1999, p. 36), and PISA is able to make such astonishing statements as:

> Students with a more advantaged socio-economic background were more likely to show a general interest in science, and this relationship was strongest in Ireland, France, Belgium and Switzerland. One significant feature of a student's background was whether they had a parent in a science-related career. (OECD, 2007a, p. 6)

Or:

> On average across OECD countries, around one-third of all variation in student performance (33%) was between schools, but this varied widely from one country to another. In Germany and the partner country Bulgaria, performance variation between schools was about twice the OECD average. It was over one and a half times the average in the Czech Republic, Austria, Hungary, the Netherlands, Belgium, Japan and Italy, and the partner countries Slovenia, Argentina and Chile. In most of these countries, the grouping or tracking of students affected this result. (OECD, 2007a, p. 4)

Thus it is that PISA, like a modern-day Pythia, is able to be all-knowing, speaking anonymously, distantly and matter-of-factly about students' interests, parents' qualifications, the efficiencies of school systems and the calibre of teachers, and to offer policy direction, set standards and encourage countries to aspire to these standards.

From 'World' to 'Word'

Although we have been following our PISA guides diligently, we are hard put to pinpoint precisely at which point the magical transformation from 'world' to 'word' occurs. When did the world become graspable and knowable? When did it become translatable into those much-trusted league tables, and the many pages of data? Like Latour in Boa Vista, we, too, find there is no single moment when this occurred. Instead, we have a chain of translations—from 'knowledge for life' to three domains of knowledge, from years of school learning to a few test items, from millions of students to a few representatives, from the efficiency of school systems to performance on a few test items. At every stage, the path can be traced back. Codes can be reversed to recover raw data. Data can be traced to countries, regions, schools and students. Test items can be traced back to the framework that so valiantly regulated them. Translations can be reversed to find the original questions.

> An essential property of this chain is that it must remain *reversible*. The succession of stages must be traceable, allowing for travel in both directions. If the chain is interrupted at any point, it ceases to transport the truth—ceases, that is, to produce, to construct, to trace, and to conduct it. *The word "refer-ence" designates the quality of the chain in its entirety*, and no longer *adequatio rei et intellectus*. Truth-value circulates here like electricity through a wire, so long as this circuit is not interrupted. (Latour, 1999, p. 69, original emphases)

Good scientific practice is about ensuring that the chain of translations is reversible, and about maintaining re-traceability.

Engaging in a 'Politics of Fact'

Like all science, PISA knowledge is a 'strange imbroglio of politics, science, technology, markets, values, ethics, facts' (Latour, 1999, p. 19). It is neither a bald and accurate representation of some 'reality out there', nor a matter of someone's 'standpoint' or imagination; it is performative, 'a collective experimentation about what humans and non-humans are together able to swallow or to withstand' (p. 20). PISA knowledge is a fabrication—but that is what *makes* it real, what gives it relevance, what adds to its validity.

Noteworthy in this 'collective experimentation' is the 'collective' itself. Understanding science as a heterogeneous achievement highlights the role of the material in truth-making. Often appearing non-controversial and benign, non-humans have been as ubiquitous, agentic and political as the humans in this production of reality. Frameworks acted as gatekeepers. Mathematical models pronounced judgements. Inscriptions prescribed and controlled. Booklets represented student knowledge. To be alert to the politics of things is to recognise new spaces for intervention.

Understanding reality as assemblage helps us to avoid treating phenomena as either given or determining. If PISA appears to speak with confidence and authority, with its air of universality, exhorting countries to 'measure up' against its standards, it is because a chain of translations have moved it from a position of hesitation to one of assurance. It has mapped the world, ordered knowledge and disciplined actors into taking up their assigned positions at regular intervals. It has coded, classified and marked people and concepts, and produced new and interesting associations. But what appears to be a monolith, a solid body of knowledge, is as a matter of traceable practices. As Law explains, ANT's ontological stance makes it possible for us to:

> ... refuse to be overawed by seemingly large systems, and the seeming onto-logical unity of the world enacted by large systems. It is, instead, to make the problem smaller, or better, to make it more specific. (Law, 2008, p. 637)

This study was prompted by the faith placed in PISA knowledge both by the OECD and by governments of some countries. It was motivated by concern that 'scientific evidence' is viewed by many policy makers today as a neutral and apolitical representation of reality, a weapon against prejudice. The use of scientific evidence has come to be seen as a hallmark of integrity in policy making. Asserting that PISA is no more or less than the sum of its practices is not to discredit the knowledge it produces; on the contrary, '*the more connected a science* is to the rest of the collective, the *better* it is, the more accurate, the more verifiable, the more solid (Latour, 1999, p. 18). Questions such as 'is it real or constructed?' deflect attention from practical issues. ANT's amodern stance avoids getting caught up in unproductive defence or debunking. By avoiding the 'science wars', Latour reminds us, 'facts and artifacts can be part of many other conversations, much less bellicose, much more productive, and, yes, much friendlier' (Latour, 1999, p. 23). Most importantly, understanding truths as 'factishes' (Latour, 1999), as being neither facts nor naïve beliefs but results of collective experimentation, draws our attention to the provisional nature of knowledge. For Latour,

> The reason one should always beware of factishes is that their consequences are unforseen, the moral order fragile, the social one unstable. (p. 288)

This being the case, he advocates 'care and caution' in dealing with knowledge—both in its use and in its fabrication. For those involved in the production of PISA, such an understanding would highlight their responsibility as assemblers of this knowledge. Knowing that different practices and different devices would lead to different results with different consequences means that those that produce PISA must take responsibility for the consequences of the knowledge they produce; the truths they produce do not predate their efforts. Rather than speak with the authority of Apollo, or with detachment, as if on behalf of Science, the producers of PISA might foreground PISA's fragility and provisionality rather than its validity and certainty. Given that PISA knowledge is at least as much fabrication as fact, care and caution are also necessary on the part of those who use PISA knowledge. Policy makers might have more modest expectations of scientists and less naïve trust in the ability of science to produce accurate, neutral and detached 'evidence'.

The scope of this paper is modest—given the enormous faith placed in statistical evidence such as PISA by education policy makers, I attempt to interrupt the view that scientific evidence is a representation of pre-existing reality. By providing a close-up view of how such knowledge is performed, I demonstrate it to be a 'matter of concern' rather than a 'matter of fact,' and thus engage in what Potter (2008) terms 'a politics of fact'. For Latour, '[t]he critic is not the one who debunks, but the one who assembles ... the one who offers the participants arenas in which to gather' (Latour, 2004, p. 246). By opening up 'scientific evidence' as a controversy, a 'matter of concern,' I provide a reminder, after Law (2008), that there is room for 'interference'.

> The question becomes: how to interfere in and diffract realities in particular locations to generate more respectful and less dominatory alternatives. How to *trope*, to bend versions of the real, to strengthen desirable realities that would otherwise be weak. (Law, 2008, p. 637)

'Interference' is a productive and optimistic engagement with phenomena. Interference could take the form of arguing for 'an ecology of practices' (Stengers, 2005) which encourages a transdisciplinary approach, affording no monopoly to any one science to make truth claims. Or it might highlight the multiplicities that lie within, and seek 'to work within and upon difference, to make differences' (Law, 2008, citing Mol 1999) and thus perform what Mol (1999) calls 'ontological politics'. When PISA—and indeed science itself—is relieved of the burden of representing prior truths, important questions about it moral and social order can raised.

Notes

1. The study Trends in International Mathematics and Science Study (TIMSS) was already in place before PISA was devised, and many OECD countries already participated in TIMSS and continue to do so. In the late 1990s, however, there appears to have been a falling out between OECD and IEA (International Association for the Evaluation of Educational Achievement), which runs TIMSS, leading to the establishment of PISA.
2. Each survey emphasises one of these three areas by turn (major domain), while including fewer items on the other two (minor domains).
3. The current contract holders are a consortium led by the Australian Council for Educational Research (ACER), and with the National Institute for Educational Measurement (CITO) of the Netherlands, WESTAT and the Educational Testing Service (ETS) in the US, and the National Institute for Educational Policy Research (NIER) in Japan (OECD, 2006, p. 16)
4. PISA was added as part of the 'outcomes' measures to the indicators that began to be developed at this time. The first PISA survey was conducted in 2000.
5. A number of studies have examined PISA against its own claims—these are collected in a volume titled *PISA According to PISA—Does PISA Keep What it Promises?* (Hopman & Brinek, 2007), available at http://www.univie.ac.at/pisaaccordingtopisa/pisazufolgepisa.pdf
6. Finland, of course, is the envy of the world—the country that consistently steals top honours on the PISA tests.
7. The FEGs themselves were quite small—four or five members—having a committee of 30 would have made decision-making very difficult.
8. The notion of 'objectivity' is variable. Berg & Timmermans (2000) point to a number of meanings of 'objectivity' such as ' "empirical reliability", "procedural correctness", "emotional detachment", "being true to nature" and "being without perspective" ' (pp. 767, 768). They remind us that notions of objectivity vary across scientific fields. But importantly for ANT theorists, objectivity does not refer to some inherent quality of an entity or action, as much as to the socio-material assemblage which produces it. While the individuals charged with actually doing the scoring are restricted from exercising too much 'subjective judgement', the developers of the criteria or the reference points given to the judges clearly have their subjectivity inscribed into these criteria or rating schemes. The idea that tests can be 'objective' and that objectivity is even desirable is contestable.
9. Here the word 'arbitrary' does not imply randomness or lack of reason; rather, it is about 'arbitration'—intervention, negotiation, a matter of settling on a decision.
10. Latour's description of science as a collective experimentation that depends on what the collective will 'swallow' or tolerate is well demonstrated here.
11. There were 13 booklets in PISA 2000. Four of these were answered by students with special needs, and these are often referred to separately.
12. This is another astonishing feat—by broadening the scope of the 'basket', the answer can be 'caught' even when it is off target. By being accommodating, PISA is able to ensure that it does not have to reject answers on the basis of inaccuracy. Instead, it simply converts the particular answer a student may give, and places it within a 'band' where it can mingle with others of varying accuracy, with the hope that 'it will all even out'.

References

Barry, A. (2009) Background Notes on Laboratory Studies and Actor Network Theory (unpublished lecture notes—online resource). Available at: http://weblearn.ox.ac.uk/site/socsci/ouce/uhs/fhs/spofpol/notesonlabstudies.doc (accessed 19 August 2009).

Bautier, E. & Rayou, P. (2007) What PISA Really Evaluates: Literacy or students' universes of reference?, *Journal of Educational Change*, 8, pp. 359–364.

Berg, M. & Timmermans, S. (2000) Orders and Their Others: On the constitution of universalities in medical work, *Configurations*, 8, pp. 31–61.

Bottani, N. & Walberg, H. J. (1992) Introduction: What are international education indicators for?, in: *The OECD International Education Indicators—A Framework for Analysis*, (Paris, OECD).

Bracey, G. W. (2008) The Leaning (Toppling?) Tower of PISA?, *Principal Leadership*, 9:2, pp. 49–51.

Connolly, P. (2006) Summary Statistics, Educational Achievement Gaps and the Ecological Fallacy, *Oxford Review of Education*, 32:2, pp. 235–252.

Corbett, M. (2008) The Edumometer: The commodification of learning from Galton to the PISA, *Journal for Critical Education Policy Studies*, 6:1. Available at: http://www.jceps.com/index.php?pageID=article&articleID=125.

Gillard, J. (2008a) *Speech at the ACER Research Conference*. Paper presented at the ACER Research Conference.

Gillard, J. (2008b) Transcript—Issues COAG; National Education Agreement.

Grek, S. (2007) '*And the Winner is ...*': PISA and the construction of the European education space. Paper presented at the 'Advancing the European Education Agenda' European Education Policy Network Conference.

Grek, S., Lawn, M. & Ozga, J. (2009) *Production of OECD's 'Programme for International Student Assessment (PISA)'*, (Edinburgh, Centre for Educational Sociology, University of Edinburgh).

Haraway, D. (1988) Situated Knowledges: The science question in feminism and the privilege of partial perspective, *Feminist Studies*, 14:3, pp. 575–599.

Hopman, S. & Brinek, T. G. (2007) PISA According to PISA—Does PISA Keep What It Promises? in: S. Hopman, T, G. Brinek & M. Retzl (eds), *PISA According to PISA—Does PISA Keep What It Promises?* (Berlin, Lit Verlag Dr. W. Hopf).

Latour, B. (1987) *Science in Action: How to follow scientists and engineers through society* (Cambridge, MA, Harvard University Press).

Latour, B. (1999) *Pandora's Hope: Essays on the reality of science studies* (Cambridge, MA, Harvard University Press).

Latour, B. (2004) Why Has Critique Run out of Steam? From matters of fact to matters of concern, *Critical Inquiry*, 30, pp. 225–248.

Law, J. (2007) Actor Network Theory and Material Semiotics. Available at: http://www.heterogeneities.net/publications/Law-ANTandMaterialSemiotics.pdf (accessed 25 April 2007).

Law, J. (2008) On Sociology and STS, *The Sociological Review*, 56:4, pp. 623–649.

Masters, G. (2001) *Educational Measurement Assessment Resource Kit* (Camberwell, VIC, ACER).

Mol, A. (1999) Ontological Politics: A word and some questions, in: J. Law & J. Hassard (eds), *Actor Network Theory and After* (Oxford and Keele, Blackwell and the Sociological Review).

OECD (2006) *Assessing Scientific, Reading and Mathematical Literacy—A Framework for PISA 2006* (Paris, OECD).

OECD (2007a) *PISA 2006 Science Competencies for Tomorrow's World. Volume 1: Analysis (Executive Summary)*. Available at: http://www.oecd.org/dataoecd/15/13/39725224.pdf (accessed 25 May 2008).

OECD (2007b) PISA—The OECD Program for International Student Assessment. Available at: http://www.pisa.oecd.org/dataoecd/51/27/37474503.pdf (accessed 23 Feb 2007).

OECD (2009) *PISA 2006 Technical Report* (Paris, Programme for International Student Assessment OECD).

Potter, E. (2008) A Sustainable Practice: Rethinking nature in cultural research, *Continuum: Journal of Media & Cultural Studies*, 22:2, pp. 171–178.

Simola, H. (2005) The Finnish Miracle of PISA: Historical and sociological remarks on teaching and teacher education, *Comparative EducationI* 41:4, pp. 455–470.

Skillbeck, M. (2006) Essay Review: Educating the knowledge society. *Minerva*, 44, pp. 89–101.

Stack, M. (2006) Testing, Testing, Read All About It: Canadian press coverage of the PISA results, *Candian Journal of Education*, 29:1, pp. 49–69.

Steiner-Khamsi, G. (2006) The Economics of Policy Borrowing and Lending: A study of late adopters, *Oxford Review of Education*, 32:5, pp. 665–678.

Stengers, I. (2005) Introductory Notes on an Ecology of Practices, *Cultural Studies Review*, 11:1.

Suchman, L. (2000) Located Accountabilities in Technology Production. Available at: http://www.comp.lancs.ac.uk/sociology/soc039ls.htm (accessed 7 June 2009).

Wright, B. D. & Stone, M. H. (1979) *Best Test Design* (Chicago, Mesa Press).

5

Assembling the 'Accomplished' Teacher: The performativity and politics of professional teaching standards

Dianne Mulcahy

Introduction

For a decade or more, successive Australian governments have taken a variety of initiatives towards improving the quality of teaching and learning in schools. Part of neo-liberal education policy reform, professional teaching standards are seen to have an important role to play in producing this improvement. Driven by a diverse range of concerns including the demand for greater teacher and school accountability, the perceived need to improve the quality of teaching and assure this quality, the interest in the link between quality teaching and quality learning and the introduction of teacher performance appraisal (and, currently, renewed discussion about teacher performance-based pay), these standards have been developed nationally by professional associations and state education authorities.

Professional teaching standards are taken to define accomplished or high-quality teaching. They are one of the main tools through which policy makers and education authorities, in many countries, including Australia, hope to make teaching practice less variable, more reliable and increasingly effective. Typically, teaching standards seek to articulate what is valued about teaching and describe the critical features of what teachers *know*, *believe* and are able to *do*. Providing opportunities for teachers to open up the 'black box' of teaching and learning, and explore these reciprocal processes in an explicit way, they constitute a key element in nations' aspirations to develop world-class standards of classroom teaching.

In this article, I explore the character and politics of professional teaching standards giving particular attention to their role in producing a certain sort of teacher identity. I argue that a unitary, stable conception of standards tends to prevail in the fields of education research and education policy and that this conception can serve to conceal the circumstances (social, material, discursive, political) that give rise to them, as well as efface the 'invisible work' that everyday actors such as teachers and learners do in order to sustain them. Adopting Pickering's (1995, p. 351) framing of scientific practice, I contrast two different idioms for thinking about and studying standards, the representational and the performative. The former idiom casts standards as a 'technology'[1] for discovering and describing *pre-existing* realities of teaching; the latter idiom casts them as relationally *enacted* in classroom and other localisable practices.

Researching Education Through Actor-Network Theory, First Edition. Edited by Tara Fenwick and Richard Edwards.
Chapters © 2012 The Authors. Book compilation © 2012 Philosophy of Education Society of Australasia.

Using data collected as part of an Australian Research Council project on (i) the relationship between professional teaching standards and teacher professional learning,[2] and (ii) the development of a specific set of professional standards, standards for teaching school geography, I address the issue of how the representational idiom of standards has become so authoritative that it readily eclipses other ways to think and 'do' standards. Addressing this issue empirically, and with an eye to the responsibility that I, as a researcher, have to account for my performative practices—my knowledge making moves[3]—I introduce three project locales or empirical contexts in which this development is taking place. I show that a different reality for teaching standards *and* for accomplished teaching presents in each of these locales. In so showing, I ask: what sorts of things *are* standards; how are they generated within processes of a research project, and can there ever be a unitary, stable conception and practice of standards, teaching and 'accomplished teacher'?

Drawing on the distinctive semiotic perspective of actor-network theory (Latour, 2005; Law, 1992, 2009; Law & Hassard, 1999) in which material agency is accented, and taking seriously its idea[4] that objects, like human subjects, will take different forms in different places and practices (Law, 2002; Mol, 2002; Mol & Law, 1994), I ask the seemingly simple question: 'where *are* standards?' towards conducting an *ontological inquiry* and argue, after Moser (2008, p. 99) that if entities such as teaching standards are enacted differently in different socio-material practices and arrangements, then it becomes important to explore the politics of the practices and arrangements that prevail.

The article is organised into three substantive sections. In section two, after some preliminary definitional work, I sketch some modes of storying standards and standards development as emerging fields of study and practice. I follow this sketch with a summary of the central tenets of actor-network theory (ANT) as an intellectual tradition that provides a performative perspective on teaching standards and accomplished teaching. Next, in section three, a national empirical study of the development of professional standards for teaching geography in Australian schools is outlined and details describing the empirical methods used to investigate, and simultaneously develop, these standards are given. Data from this study are worked via the telling of three stories of teaching standards that feature the locales or empirical contexts in which this development is taking place. In section four, I conclude by discussing the distinctiveness of the contribution of ANT to studies of standards and subjectivity (the 'accomplished' teacher) and examining some of the implications of the politics it promotes for standards-based education reform. In keeping with ANT, I attend most particularly to materialities and material politics (Law & Mol, 2008).

Clearing Some Definitional Ground: Standards as Epistemic Objects

Writing in the context of educational reform, Sykes and Plastrik (1993, p. 4) define standards as 'a tool for rendering appropriately precise the making of judgements and decisions in the context of shared meanings and values'. This definition would seem to suggest that standards are technologies (tools) in the service of broader social and cultural agendas. Emphasis is placed on the role that standards play rather than on the nature of standards themselves. This has the effect, I would argue, of naturalising and neutralising the content of standards—the knowledge that they embed and the power relations that they are caught up in and can catch others up in (eg. standardization, surveillance, regulation). It also has the effect of eclipsing the idea that objects such as standards are *epistemic*: standards are not only the objects of knowledge practice but also objects *in* knowledge practice, here, the practice of articulating what is valued about teaching and describing the critical features of what teachers know, believe and do.

In my preferred definition of standards, a standard is 'any set of agreed-upon rules for the production of (textual or material) objects' (Bowker & Star, 1999, p. 13). In this sociological understanding of standards, stress is placed not only on rules (which, as we know from the later Wittgenstein, do not include their own applications), but also on performativity. Standards do not simply describe pre-existing realities such as accomplished teaching practice or accomplished teachers; they actively produce them. They are 'significant participants in knowledge work' (Ewenstein & Whyte, 2009, p. 9). Across the terrain of these two definitions, attention shifts from social and cultural processes ('the making of judgements ... in the context of shared meanings') to objects (here 'rules') and their agency and effects. Influenced as I am by actor-network theory, which, as one of its founders claims, invites its practitioners to 'predominantly *think* through materials' (Law, 2008, p. 629, emphasis in original), I maintain that this is an important shift. 'A focus on objects brings practice into view and the rich material contexts and dense social relations in which production takes place. An analytical interest in objects also reveals their centrality to the various processes and practices of learning and knowing' (Ewenstein & Whyte, 2009, p. 8).

What Counts as a Standard?: Orthodoxies and other Stories

In what follows, I tell two tales of teaching standards: teaching standards as first and foremost a research and policy strategy for implementing education reform—ontological shift—teaching standards as a process of knowledge making in everyday teaching practice. A comparison is drawn between two different idioms for knowing (I should add 'doing') standards and their development. Munro argues that: 'against a too-rigid insistence on consistency, might be placed the device of comparison, a juxtaposition of difference. In terms of analysis, there is sometimes more contrast to be gained from moving "in-between" competing divisions, rather than choosing one over another' (1997, p. 6). In what follows, I attempt to gain this contrast.

Standards as Knowledge Statements: A Realist Tale

Cast in a representational idiom, teaching standards aim at achieving a correct representation of the reality of what teachers know, believe and are able to do. What might be called 'Big S' standards assume the form of statements structured in a particular way and subsequently published in documents that can circulate widely, so producing their apparent universality. Thus leading standards researchers in Australia, when commenting on the character of well-written standards, say 'the standard is context free, in the sense that it describes a practice that most agree accomplished ... teachers should follow no matter where the school is. By definition, a professional standard applies to all contexts in which teachers work' (Ingvarson & Rowe, 2008, p. 18).

Told principally by policymakers and regulatory bodies such as teacher registration authorities, this tale takes it that teaching is the type of activity that can and should be captured in standards. 'Standards were invented to develop the capacity to have direct knowledge and access to what was previously opaque' (Popkewitz, 2004, p. 245). Brought together at a single site—inscribed often on a single sheet of paper—standards are conceived as the result of the consensual thinking of groups such as teaching professionals, system officials or field-specific academics and organised into categories and sub-categories (eg. capabilities, descriptors). By way of illustration, the National Professional Standards for Teachers of History in Australia read:

Professional knowledge

1. Teachers know their subject
2. Teachers know how students learn to be historically literate
3. Teachers know their students

Professional practice

1. Teachers plan for effective learning
2. Teachers establish and maintain a challenging and effective learning environment
3. Teachers assess and review student learning in history

Professional engagement

1. Teachers demonstrate a commitment to the teaching and learning of history
2. Teachers continue to learn
3. Teachers are active members of the professional and wider community
   http://www.historystandards.com/content/view/25/37

In the continuing debate about the nature of a knowledge base for teaching (see, for example, Hiebert, Gallimore, & Stigler, 2002), teaching standards can be viewed as the practical articulation of the knowledge base of the profession. As Yinger and Hendricks-Lee (2000, p. 95) state, 'For this knowledge base to be created, a discourse language must be created that connects abstract knowledge and theory to the demands and realities of practice. Research and knowledge-based standards can serve in this manner by creating a shared and public "language of practice" ' (Yinger, 1987).

Notably here, knowledge is conceived as external to practice—'this abstract knowledge base is generated ... primarily by the academy'—and standards are constituted as neutral carriers of this knowledge. 'Standards, in and of themselves, are broad and benign. It is in the use of standards that conflicts and tensions arise' (ibid., p. 99). The assumption is made that standards are knowledge representations. Importantly, ' "representation" and "reality" are separated by a universal line of demarcation, with the latter prior and the former more or less adequately descriptive' (Oppenheim, 2007, p. 489). Modernist epistemologies tend to support the idea of teaching standards as *tools* that accurately report on the realities of teaching practice or serve to capture these realities in a more or less adequate way. In so doing, they miss the complexities of standards, their irreducible elements, things that signify but do not necessarily sum—that are not necessarily able to be described or are only partially discursively available. The tool version of standards also misses their socio-political agenda-setting.

Standards as Knowledge Practices: A Performative Tale

The conceptual basis of current standards research and development work seems to have taken *representation* as its central focus and tends to leave those who create the representations largely out of the picture.[5] As Pickering (1995, p. 6) comments, 'within the representational idiom, people and things tend to appear as shadows of themselves'. If standards are construed in their performativity, their developers and the development process, including the performative role in standards of language itself, are part of the account. As Barad (2003, p. 802) has it, 'the move towards performative alternatives to representationalism shifts the focus from questions of correspondence between descriptions and reality (e.g. do they mirror nature or culture?) to matters of practices/doings/actions'.

Cast in a performative idiom, standards are knowledge (and identity) making processes performed in classroom and other localisable practices. Here, the assumption is made 'that knowledge is produced at the point of performance of situated understandings' (Verran *et al.*, 2007). Accordingly, standards are no longer taken to be a tool for teachers (and others) to use; they are rather an *activity* in which people might participate. Actor-network theory shows the way towards a fully performative understanding of teaching standards and teacher identity. 'The basic metaphysics of the actor-network is that we should think of science (and technology and society [and standards and subjectivity]) as a field of human and nonhuman (material) agency' (Pickering, 1995, p. 11). Taking the entanglements of these disparate agencies as given, it credits the idea that representations—descriptions of accomplished practice—and realities—accomplished practice—come into being together. Descriptions are performances and no description is ever entirely innocent (Law & Singleton, 2000).

Taking the performative turn in standards research affords a non-hierarchical way of thinking about difference. It invites the dissolution of dichotomies such as representation and reality, theory and practice, technical tool and human activity. It also affords suspension of the means-ends production model of standards whereby the features of good teaching are described and the descriptions are handed off 'finished' into the field. Massey (1999) calls this way of thinking relational thinking, explaining thus: '(Relational thinking) is, in part, an attempt to reimagine the either/or constructions of binary thinking (where the only relations are negative ones of exclusion) and to recognise the important elements of interconnection which go into the construction of any identity' (*ibid.*, p. 12). This way of thinking—or, more broadly, relationality—is central to the concerns of ANT.

Travelling with Actor-Network Theory: 'It's Practice All the Way Down'[6]

Actor-network theory is a theory about *how* knowledge comes to be produced and takes materiality to be 'tangible knowledge' (Gherardi, 2006). As Law (1994) has it, ANT looks at the resources that are mobilised to establish an object of knowledge: people, devices, texts, decisions, organisations, inter-organisational relations. More recently, he describes it as 'a disparate family of material-semiotic tools, sensibilities and methods of analysis that treat everything in the social and natural worlds as a continuously generated effect of the webs of relations within which they are located' (2009, p. 141). Early ANT analysis was concerned to understand how heterogeneous entities are drawn together to establish objects of knowledge. This analysis was undertaken by putting concepts such as 'network' and 'translation' to work. Thus, the creation of relatively stable networks of relations was traced by following processes of translation—the displacement or shifting out of the interests and concerns of one network into that of another. Challenging the idea that knowledge is not the only thing being contested in instances of controversy or concern, contemporary ANT inquiries tend to ask: 'What if that which knowledge represents—reality—is also (at times) conflicting? What if multiple knowledges reflect not only varying positions but, in certain situations, a multiple ontology?' (Carolan, 2004, p. 498).

Taking an 'ontological turn' in the late 1990s, ANT now entertains the idea that 'there are different and not necessarily consistent realities' (Law, 2007, p. 600)—we do not necessarily live in a single natural or material reality. For ANT, the debate is no longer 'about epistemology—about how to see (a single) reality. Instead it is about ontology, about what is real, what is out there' and how reality is achieved (*ibid.*). The assumption is made that nothing has reality, or form, outside its performance in webs of relations with performances being defined as 'material processes, practices, which take place day by day and minute by minute' (Law & Singleton, 2000, p. 775). The turn to performance has been taken in various disciplinary fields (eg. human geography, cultural studies, contemporary political theory). ANT's version of this turn affords attention to *materiality* and *multiplicity* and, in so doing, promotes investigation of ontological difference.

> Since performances are specific, this also leads to multiplicity, so that what appears to be one thing (an 'object,' 'working,' 'knowledge') may be understood as a set of related performances. More strongly, it suggests that abstraction (including abstract knowledge) is a performance, something enacted in specific locations that has to be reenacted in other locations in further performances if it is to carry. This has all sorts of implications. One is that things don't come to rest in a single form once agreement, or what is called 'closure,' is achieved. They rumble on and on, as it were, noisy and noisome (*ibid.*).

A salutary story for teaching standards! In holding to the idea that reality does not precede practices but is made through them, ANT attends to the idea that practices have a political life. 'Practices organize and reproduce the distribution of power, knowledge, and the inequalities that go with them' (Nicolini, Gherardi, & Yanow, 2003, p. 24). They have built-in normativities, contributing to 'some worlds-in-progress but not to others' (Moser, 2008, p. 99). The question becomes which worlds we want practices to make. As performative knowledge-making, research too is engaged in ontological work and, as Verran *et al.* (2007, p. 129) claim, 'accounting it should also be performative'. The methodology of material semiotics propels reflexive attention to the material practices through which one's research evidence is gathered and one's claims are produced. Accordingly, in the fieldwork tales that follow, I attempt to show (at least some of) the workings of world- and knowledge-making in the standards project under consideration—take the reader to the locales and practices in which the standards and the project knowledge of standards are (co)produced.

The Project in Question: Data and Method Assemblage[7]

The first empirical phase of the project described (performed) here was concerned to study what 'accomplished' geography teaching *is* by documenting what geography teach- ers, who are deemed accomplished, *do*. Data were sourced from teachers and students via video recordings of accomplished teaching[8] with identification of accomplished teachers being made by way of purposeful sampling. Thus, members of the Australian Geography Teachers' Association and its affiliates, the peak professional associations for school geography in Australia, were invited to nominate teachers who are widely regarded professionally, using various criteria including reputation for accomplishment within the field of geographic education, years of experience teaching school geography, teaching qualifications, etc.

In an effort to 'capture' the specificities of practice, including the flow of teacher action and embodied judgement, the approach adopted uses technically complex methods for video recording classrooms and supplementing the video records with post-lesson video- stimulated interviews with students and the teacher.[9] To date, ten case studies (20 lessons altogether) have been conducted in eight schools (government and non-government; metropolitan and non-metropolitan) in three major Australian states. In all cases, video recordings were made over the course of a sequence of two lessons, each lasting for approximately fifty minutes. The first of the fieldwork tales below concerns one of these case studies.

The second empirical phase of the project, which is ongoing, seeks to study what 'accomplished' geography teaching *is* by documenting what geography teachers, at different stages of their career, *say* about accomplished practice, with particular attention to samples of practice from the video-recordings made as part of the first project phase.[10] This phase involves the conduct of focus groups or teacher panel meetings in five Australian states. Meeting twice over six months, panels of practising geography teachers (64 teachers altogether) are tasked with reviewing video excerpts and related data (e.g. samples of students' work) and responding to a series of semi-structured questions designed to identify elements of accomplished practice, towards the development of standards for teaching school geography. The further fieldwork tales told below—tales two and three—are set within two 'contexts' of this development, firstly, a panel consul- tation *website* comprising various data files; and secondly, teacher *panel meetings* where data collected from twenty-five panel members are discussed.

In tracing the shifting relations of standards through a research project that spans different contexts or locales, I tell a story of teaching standards and teacher subjectivity as multiple and partial. The development of professional standards for teaching geogra- phy in Australian schools serves here as a kind of case study for advancing a way of thinking about teaching standards as not only written representations but also material practices which transform, and are transformed by, identities. Place locations and names of teachers and students have been altered for reasons of confidentiality.

Teaching and Standards of Teaching: Performative Tales from the Field

A Classroom Tale: Standards as Embodied[11] Practice

My first empirical context concerns a classroom set within a large, private, all boys' metropolitan school. Deemed by her peers to be a highly accomplished geography teacher, Caroline is about to commence a class in which the Year Nines are to be introduced to Geelong, Australia's largest regional municipality and 'Home of the Cats', an Australian Rules football team which, after forty-four years, has finally managed to win a premiership. Teaching at an all boys' school where sport, most particularly football, has a large and fanatical following,[12] she aims to take 'geography a little bit to a different level, so looking at the geography of sport and then we are going to actually map where the goals were kicked and the behinds were kicked using the choropleth technique and then we are going to do a ray diagram (looking at) where the players come from, to go to play for Geelong'.

The classroom version of teaching and standards of teaching provides a strong sense of standards as an *activity* in which people participate as well as of the role and contribution of knowledge practices that are not necessarily state-able as standards. I will take each of these in turn.

In conjunction with the boys, Caroline is engaged in standards setting, articulating the norms or rules that are used in school geography for determining levels of achievement in this subject. Importantly, these norms are heterogeneous; they involve an *entanglement* of behavioural, material and cognitive elements. Parsing the lesson,[13] Caroline begins a sequence in this way:

> Looking at the handout please gentlemen, take that in front of you. We're going to work through the different questions quite slowly today so that we're really learning the correct way to do some answers and the first one we are going to look at is the map which is labelled A, alright, so it's showing the location of Melbourne and then Geelong. It's the very first map; could you all look at that please. [It's labelled] A. Now if we look at our handout, the written answer one, it says [reads aloud]: 'This data broadsheet introduces us to a range of what we call geographic media'. Now in Year 12, they have to have a range of media in order to present their work. And they're tested at Year 12 and 11, we test the ways that they can present information. So I've given you a selection of media here to show data about Geelong. So look through the data A-S, which you've just done, to get a feel for the characteristics of Geelong. Now the first one A is what we call a thematic map. Looking at the map A [reads aloud]: 'Name the main land use which is shown on the map'. Now where would a good place be to find that answer if you're looking at a map? [Student response in the background.] The legend. Have a look at the legend, sometimes it's called the key and what is it actually telling us?

Behavioural elements such as 'Looking at the handout please gentlemen' are directed at keeping the class on task and focusing attention on salient features of the content under consideration. Cognitive elements such as the selection of media that Caroline has made by way of a data broadsheet conform largely to existing versions of professional standards which are 'usually organised by categories which represent the critical elements that must be brought together for accomplished teaching' (Teaching Australia, 2007, p. 8), the critical elements here being teacher preparation/planning, teacher subject knowledge, teacher commitment to student learning, and so on. Material objects (the handout) and practices ('Looking at the map') carry the categorical; standards don't exist in the abstract.

Standards are everywhere apparent—'Come on you guys, hurry up and go to class'; they are built and practised—'We're going to work through the different questions quite slowly today so that we're really learning the correct way to do some answers'; and they are achieved by both teacher and students—'I think that's why these lessons take a long time on the questions because we're trying to be as concise as we can'. They also demand physical work, certainly on the part of the teacher, who regularly walks around and helps those who need assistance. Bodies (and the spaces they inhabit) are central to achieving accomplished teaching. Teaching and standards of teaching are not read off a lesson plan or a set of standards statements, rather they are enacted. And their enactments are 'material processes, practices, which take place day by day and minute by minute' (Law & Singleton, 2000, p. 775).

Tracing teaching standards-in-practice affords knowing teaching and standards of teaching in practical (socio-material) and performative ways. Other versions of standards ill afford this knowledge. Thus formal standards statements tend not to acknowledge the embodied judgements that teachers make in their everyday work such as is evidenced in Caroline's shift in the above when explaining the conduct of geographic education in Year 12: 'Now in Year 12, they have to have a range of media in order to present their work ... . So I've given you a selection of media here'. These judgements are contingent upon the shifting circumstances of teaching and specific to classroom events. As Beckett and Hager (2000) comment, the making of practical judgements is discretionary and contextually sensitive. As I read these data, Caroline is taking an opportunity to shape the subjectivity of the Year 9s. Implying the importance of school geography in the senior years, she aims to steer their curriculum choices, fashion a future for them as would-be geographers. Making a seeming diversion from her teaching text, she deems that a connection between the work and learning worlds of different levels of student should be made, serving as it might to motivate the Year 9s with regard to learning to work with a range of geographic media. Caroline's judgment is made in the *flow of action*, exemplifying the idea 'that knowledge is produced at the point of performance of situated understandings' (Verran *et al.*, 2007).

In line with teacher judgment, teacher humour and disposition (felt intensities, teacher passion) can be considered critical features of what teachers know, believe and do. As the data that follow imply, each acts to produce the practice of accomplished teaching and standards of teaching. Thus, upon initially receiving their copy of the data broadsheet circulated in class, a pair of boys draw attention to an image of a premiership poster[14] on this broadsheet:

Pointing at the image of the poster repeated on the broadsheet, David says to his partner at the double desk—'She had to put that in, didn't she'.
Commentary on the poster continues:
David: Miss, is that really necessary?
Caroline: Absolutely ... necessary and I've put it in twice just to reinforce the fact that Geelong won in 2007.
Zac: Why?
Caroline: Because we've been waiting a *very* long time!

A self-described 'Cats' tragic', Caroline performs a distinctive form of teaching work: 'Good teaching is to do with teachers' values, identities, moral purposes, attitudes to learning (their own as well as those of their students), their caring and commitment ... their enthusiasm and their passion' (Day, 2004, pp. 15–16). The curriculum materials that she has prepared afford an opportunity to extend students' understanding of the subject matter and consolidate relationships with them through a show of emotion vis-à-vis her team's long awaited success. Material processes (poster preparation, teacher gesture and vocal emphasis—'Because we've been waiting a *very* long time') make dispositional dimensions of teaching, and the standards that they imply, apparent and consequently contestable: 'Miss, is that really necessary'? The social and dispositional dimensions of accomplished teaching emerge explicitly at interview, with one of Caroline's students commenting: 'She's like a good teacher, laid back, like she's serious in a way but she can have a joke'. Having a joke (and tolerating tongue in cheek comments from the students) enters into the organisation and production of the subjectivity of accomplished teacher and the practice and standards of accomplished teaching. These specificities are, so to say, the hinterland of accomplished teaching, *embodied practices* which carry content of a context sensitive kind—content which does not lend itself to codification.

A Tale of a Panel Consultation Website: Standards as Quasi Statements

My second empirical context concerns a consultation website on which samples of accomplished geography teaching gathered from the video case studies, and comments on this teaching by the teachers and students concerned, can be accessed. Like the 'embodied' version of teaching and standards of teaching, the consultation website provides a strong sense of standards as an *activity* in which people—here practising teachers who are taking part in panel meetings—participate; this participation however, occurs at a remove from classroom practice. In being asked to review samples of teaching practice, knowledge of standards and the standards themselves are not being produced at the point of performance of situated understandings (Verran *et al.*, 2007). Rather, this knowledge is a product of the processing of various case data—video, image, text, audio—that teacher participants respond to. The principal material practice in play is a viewing diary which these participants are invited to keep, towards the production of an account of accomplished teaching. As shown in Figure 1, they make a choice of samples for review from a menu of samples, each of which features a key geographic concept or practice, for example, the concept of relative location (sample 2) or population growth (sample 6a); the practice of topographic mapping (sample 7) or field-sketching (sample 3).

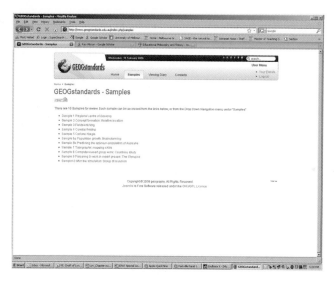

Figure 1: Samples page: teacher panel consultation website

Having made their selection of samples and processed the data, the teacher participants are invited to complete and submit a diary entry for each selection. These submissions are 'scaffolded' (a further material practice) using a set of questions, the chief of which for present purposes is: 'What counts as accomplished teaching in this sample'?

Using 'Sample 1: Regional centre of Geelong'—the case data collected in Caroline's classroom and storied above—as an illustrative example, a small number of responses to this question has been selected randomly to give a sense of teachers' submissions:

T2: 'Introducing data and how to read it. I believe geography teachers are able to draw kids' attention to data by that constant reference to figure numbers, asking what the map/graph is showing and the legend'.

T4: 'Knowledge of the higher order Geography skills and techniques which underpin this task.
Allowing students to discover what they think is important in the data.
Comfort with the open discussion and allowing some of her passion to show (Cats supporter!)'.

T3: 'Use of students' prior knowledge, supplementary questioning to encourage deeper thinking. Catering for different learners—use of verbal, written and visual cues. Involvement of most members of the class in the initial discussion contributes to engagement. Scaffolding of a task, which can be accomplished on a variety of levels catering for individual abilities. Setting students a challenge—find something new or interesting'.

T6: 'The teacher has been able to use a topic of interest to her students as the vehicle through which to promote the development of geospatial skills.
The teacher has presented a range of geographic media from which students are able to build their own understanding of the importance of Geelong as a regional centre. The teacher has collected authentic data on a location that a number of her students are reasonably familiar with'.

T1: 'Preparation of interesting & relevant materials. Teacher engages the students'.

T5: 'Relaxed personality reflecting confidence of knowing the educational limits of her class as well as the actual teaching material'.

T7: 'Content—geographic and skills/concepts based. Timing and presentation—materials prepared and learning planned. Preparation of own materials to allow for own teaching style and needs of students'.

At this point in the project, standards are *quasi statements*: statements that characterise rather than categorise accomplished practice. While well on the way to becoming generalised statements about accomplished geography teaching—'geography teachers are able to draw kids' attention to data'—this version of standards is not context free. A strong sense of the specificity of practices is provided and the dispositional dimensions of accomplished teaching are in view: 'Relaxed personality reflecting confidence of knowing the educational limits of her class'; 'Comfort with the open discussion and allowing some of her passion to show (Cats supporter!)'. The key material process of completing a viewing diary implies the idea of standards as an *account* of accomplished teaching. Nevertheless, this account is *grounded* in case studies. As quasi statements, standards ill afford the achievement of epistemic scale. Enacted in other locations and socio-material practices however, standards readily scale 'out' and 'up'.

A Composite Tale of Teacher Panels: Standards As Statements

Tracing the movement of standards from the classroom to the profession at large brings me to the third locale in which the standards under study here are presently being produced—that is, teacher panel meetings (16 meetings altogether) in major Australian states. To date, three groups of geography teachers (25 teachers altogether) have met to engage in discussions about elements of accomplished geography teaching using video excerpts from the case data collected in classrooms. Held at various sites, the first meeting of each panel runs for approximately five hours with the last hour being given over to identification of elements of accomplished geography teaching. By way of illustration, a small selection of these elements, as identified by the teachers above, is as follows:

Predisposition to geographical content knowledge. Connecting with here and now teachable moments	Making connections with other disciplines using a geography lens	Incorporation of spatial concepts (explicit & implicit)	Able to listen, respond, encourage thinking and justification based on data and evidence
Uses classroom episodes that engage students in self directed and peer orientated learning	Uses the language and tools of the subject	Students are encouraged and supported to be active citizens in their world (either locally, nationally, globally)	Fieldwork
Interlinking of human and natural (physical) world	Embraces the use of multi media, new technologies, spatial technologies	Professional practice is improved and maintained through targeted geographical professional development	Ability to seek to use learning technologies in ways that transform the pedagogy of geographical education

Bringing people/artefacts/the world into the classroom and taking the students into the world	Teachers see themselves as a Geographer— studies are always reflecting / using the Geographical Inquiry Approach	Selection of relevant, stimulating and suitable case studies	Incorporation of real world examples and current material/issues

Written in response to the question, 'What is it that the accomplished geography teacher does?', each of these elements is general in nature. The identified elements pertain to the professional practice of geography teaching as a whole. A distillation and 'scaling out' of the content of accomplished practice occurs—'Professional practice is improved and maintained through targeted geographical professional development'—with little reference to the 'lived' and contingent conditions of classrooms.

In one seemingly small move, a move made by way of three technologies (Shapin & Schaffer, 1985)—the *material technology* of post-it notes on which the elements of accomplished geography teaching are recorded; the *literary technology* of lists which itemise the elements and can serve to discourage expression of participant debate or disputation around them; and the *social technology* of deploying a panel of practising geography teachers who are taken to be able to testify to the character of accomplished geography teaching—standards emerge as representations of teachers' abilities, predispositions, positioning, knowledge and skills. Once organised into categories and subcategories, these representations comprise standards statements, the currently valued version of standards which can circulate widely and inform the decisions of constituencies such as policy makers and policy advisors who, in Australia, are engaged presently in establishing a national curriculum and the place of subject specialisations such as school geography in this curriculum.

Assembling the Accomplished Teacher: Whose Assemblage Counts?

The practice of teaching, identity of teacher and standards of teaching are co-assembled; they come into being together. In the first of the data stories (Lather, 1991) told above, accomplished practice, accomplished practitioner, and standards of accomplishment are intricately entwined. Teaching standards are never just paper prescriptions nor neutral representations of what teachers know, believe and are able to do but are always something more. They are material practices which are performed ... minute by minute: 'Looking at the handout please gentlemen, take that in front of you. We're going to work through the different questions quite slowly today so that we're really learning the correct way to do some answers'. Studying a set of standards in the making, I have traced how webs of social and material practices produce them. In so doing, I have questioned the way in which established stories of standards virtually make invisible how standards are achieved everyday in classrooms, that is, standards as a local, embodied and emergent practice. And, all but make inconsequential elements of knowledge which remain context specific, such as Caroline's practice of sharing a team success joke.

Again, in data stories two and three, the practice of teaching, identity of teacher and standards of teaching are co-produced. Here however, representations of accomplishment rather than enactments of accomplishment rule, resulting in a more rarefied reality of standards. Belonging to or reserved for a small select group, the contribution of students to teaching standards and the corporeal connections of teachers with students, disappear from view. On the one hand, much is gained—explicitness regarding the character of accomplished teaching and by extension, the identity of the accomplished teacher; on the other, a good deal is lost. 'The limitations to making tacit knowledge explicit are formidable ... . The probability is that "thick" tacit versions will coexist alongside "thin" explicit versions: the thick version will be used in professional practice, the thin version for justification' (Eraut, 2000, pp. 134–5). Privileging a representational function over a practical or performative one, standards emerge as a stabilised knowledge base, rather than a specific kind of practice.

Analyses of the empirical data afford a clear sense of the patterns that form with respect to standards and subjectivity. They point to radically different logics of scale and location and imply differential social consequences and effects. Thus, standards studied in classroom practice settings show the critical role that embodiment plays in student learning and the significant role of students in shaping rules of engagement in classrooms: 'Miss, is that really necessary'? In contrast, standards studied in policy/professional settings show the centrality of representations and the seminal role of stakeholders other than students. Standards are ontologically variable—here embodied knowledge practices, there abstract knowledge representations—and it is struggles around this variability that can create conditions for a renewed practice and politics of standards-based education reform.

As Cooper and Law (1995, p. 239) have it, there are two ways of knowing (I will add 'doing') human structures such as teaching standards, with each carrying the other's possibilities within itself:

> Distal thinking privileges results and outcomes, the 'finished' things or objects of thought and action. It privileges the ready-made. So the distal is what is preconceived, what appears already constituted and known, what is simplified, distilled; it's a bit like fast food—packaged for convenience and ease of consumption. Proximal thinking deals in the continuous and "unfinished"; it's what is forever approached but never attained, what is always approximated but never fully realized. The proximal is always partial and precarious, forever fated to repeat itself in an effort to reach (but never attain) completion ... . The distal stresses boundaries and separation, distinctness and clarity, hierarchy and order. The proximal manifests implication and complicity, and hence symmetry, equivalence and equivocality.

The standard story of standards privileges the distal, and tends to repress, displace or efface the proximal. It incorporates a kind of 'user model', where a preconceived representation of the user and her situation is made (Suchman, 1987). From a distal point of view, the teacher is not a standards setter or a standards developer; she is assigned an implementational role. Leaving 'distal' ways of developing standards nameless, hides other possibilities for development, as well as other developers, who, in the case of Caroline's classroom, co-exist with 'implementers' of teaching standards. In exploring standards design and development, we should attend to what has been repressed or excised, and focus up the proximal processes that generate the possibility of the distal (Cooper & Law, 1995, p. 264). In so doing, the limits of the representational idiom and of the realist ontology underscoring standards development are thrown into relief.

We cannot expect to bring all that accomplished teaching comprises to presence, certainly not in writing on paper or completing a diary entry on practice watched on a website. The standard view of standards provides a solution to the seemingly intractable problem of teaching quality by setting up a specific version of teaching standards (standards as statements) and a specific kind of teaching practice (practice that conforms to the terms of standards statements) as if they could adequately take in, and legislate for, the whole of teaching standards and teaching practice. Rather than reducing teaching practice to a specific kind of practice, acknowledging its networks (representational and performative; professional and practical) gives greater multiplicity and dimension to it. Similarly, rather than reducing standards to a singularity, acknowledging networks of standards (standards as embodied practice; standards as statements; standards as set by students) will give greater purchase on and multiplicity and dimension to them.

The Critical Contribution of Actor-Network Theory: Performative Politics

It is assumed throughout this article that we need to think and study standards differently, not escape from them. To this end, we need to abandon an 'overly representational view of knowledge' (Turnbull, 1997, p. 553). Sketching out a basis for a performative image of standards—including the 'doing'—has us more like classroom teachers and learners: the performative or enacting mode of knowledge making emerges as epistemically primary. 'Representational knowledge comes to be understood as a secondary, derived form' (Verran, 1998, p. 249). Standards are primarily to be seen not in terms of the intrinsic capabilities or potentialities of teaching professionals, or in terms of an extrinsic language of practice, but rather *performances* of teaching and learning in networks of practice.

The distinctive performative perspective of actor-network theory where the onus is on material process, lends itself well to tracing practices of performative knowledge and identity making and engaging in performative politics. Called variously ontological politics (Mol, 1999), material politics (Law & Mol, 2008) and a 'politics of what' (Mol, 2002), this is a 'politics that seeks to make use of—rather than patronising, tolerating or ignoring (or most likely all three)—differences and different ways of enacting things (be they a body, a disease, a climate, [a set of standards])' (Bingham & Hinchcliffe, 2007, p. 2). Putting this politics to work in the case under consideration here involves the promotion of different sorts of standards or different standards enactments:

> For if there are multiple realities then these may be played off against one another. Importantly, some will be preferable to others (though such judgements are themselves likely to be complex). This is the point of an ontological politics (Mol, 1999). It is to work within and upon difference, to make differences' (Law, 2008, p. 637).

Accordingly, I argue that no version of professional standards—neither the well-established version where teaching standards assume the form of statements of teachers' knowledge, skills and dispositions, nor the now less visible version where they take the form of 'wisdom of practice' performed in the everyday and embodied work of teachers—needs to and ought to prevail. Adapting Whatmore (2006) to my purposes here, this version was written out of, or more accurately, into the ancestral past of teaching standards as the practical articulation of the knowledge base of the profession. It may be time now to restore it.

In practising a politics of what, radically different ways of 'doing' accomplished teacher and standards of accomplished teaching are possible and to be preferred. One consequence of this move concerns the redistribution of accomplishment attendant on the recognition of multiple knowledge practices (social, material, representational, performative) and multiple communities (teachers, students, parents). Thinking accomplishment in this way provides a generative counter-narrative to currently established narratives of standards. It leads away from an external critique of standards-based education reform such as is sometimes made by commentators (see for example, Sachs, 2005; White *et al.*, 2004) towards more specific internal interventions in which the differences between standards practices can be played off against one another. It also challenges what might be described as a complicit relationship between teaching standards and branches of the state that sponsor them (Law, 2008).

Following an ANT-and-after trajectory, the radical difference underscoring standards is far from problematic: holding differences in tension (rather than seeking to reconcile them) provides the best possibility for achieving accomplished teaching and learning.

Notes

1. In describing the knowledge and skills that teachers should have in order to practise, teaching standards are, *par excellence*, a technology of representation. Like other representational technologies (eg. book-keeping, cartography), they allow the manipulation of objects and events at a spatial and temporal distance.

2. Spanning 2007–2010, this Linkage Project is being conducted in association with the Australian Geography Teachers' Association with affiliates in five major Australian states, including Partner Investigator status for the Geography Teachers' Association of Victoria and the teacher registration authority in Victoria (Victorian Institute of Teaching).

3. In this article, the argument is made that standards should be understood as performative knowledge and identity producing practices. Research too is performative knowledge making (Verran *et al.*, 2007). Enacting relations of responsibility in research means, among other things, that accounting it should also be performative. Accordingly, in the style of Verran *et al.* (2007), I attempt to show (at least some of) the workings of knowledge production in the standards project under consideration; take the reader to the locales and practices in which the standards and the project knowledge of standards are being (co)produced.

4. Explorations of the character of objects have been made in the field of science, technology and society (STS) for at least twenty years (Law & Singleton, 2005). Actor-network theory sits under the broad umbrella of STS. It has however, taken a particular interest in complex objects such as alcoholic liver disease (Law & Singleton, 2005), atherosclerosis (Mol, 2002) and anaemia (Mol & Law, 1994) and, in practising 'ontological radicalism' (Law & Singleton, 2005), it goes further than other parts of STS when considering the nature of the objects in the world.

5. In certain standards research and development projects, concerted efforts have been made to acknowledge and preserve the 'voice' of those doing the development work. Building on the work of the National Board for Professional Teaching Standards in the US, the project, Standards for Teachers of English Language and Literacy in Australia (STELLA), which began in Australia in1999 as a three-year research project funded by the Australian Research Council, was concerned to collect and exhibit teacher narratives towards not only telling but also 'showing' accomplished practices by Australian teachers. The purpose of the project was to develop subject specific standards for primary and secondary teachers of English that acknowledge the complexity of teaching. For a copy of the STELLA statements and their accompanying narratives see http://www.stella.org.au/

6. Invoking the teaching of Garfinkel, Latour (2005, p. 135) declares that ANT-work is 'practice all the way down'. Nothing other than close attention to the specificities of the empirical world will do.

7. There is little difference between the term assemblage (which is derived from Deleuze's notion of *agencement*) and actor-network (Law, 2004; 2009, p. 146). Thus, I use these terms interchangeably.

8. I take it that accomplishment is materially and discursively produced. The teacher/subject is produced within an institutionalised and relational use of terms such as 'accomplished', 'quality', 'advanced' and 'great'. As the National Board for Professional Teaching Standards has it, 'Every child deserves a great teacher'; see http://www.nbpts.org/

9. For each of ten classrooms in three major Australian states, two lessons, each lasting around 50 minutes, were videotaped using three cameras. One camera focused on the teacher, a second on individual students as part of a working group, and a third on the whole class as seen from the front of the room. Using as catalyst the video record from the whole class camera, with the teacher camera image inserted as a picture-in-picture image in one corner of the display, teachers were invited to make a reconstructive account of the lesson events deemed critical to student learning. Similarly, students were invited to make an account of lesson events, using as stimulus the video record from the teacher camera, with the individual students' camera image inserted as a picture-in-picture image in one corner of the display.

10. These samples were selected by members of the research team—nine people altogether, including four highly experienced geographic educators and teachers.

11. Following Thrift (2008, p. 276), I take embodiment to be an assemblage of 'flesh and accompanying objects, rather than a series of individual bodies, intersubjectively linked'.

12. Not uncommonly, for an elite, private boys' school, sport is a compulsory part of school. 'We all have to do sport at this school. We all have to give up Saturdays' (Caroline).

13. As Hiebert *et al.* (2002, p. 8) comment, 'teaching is such a complex activity that it must be parsed in some way to study it' and to undertake it. From my observation of the lesson under discussion here, this parsing involved a sequence of: initial revision of the previous lesson; question and answer eliciting prior knowledge of the new topic; formalisation and extension of this knowledge through the introduction of the data broadsheet; skill-based learning orchestrated via a handout; direct instruction using the whiteboard and so on. Each of these sequences can be understood as a pedagogic assemblage.

14. Created by the cartoonist WEG (William Ellis Green), the Grand Final souvenir poster of a cartoon cat above the caption '2007 Premiers' was made freely available by the *Sunday Herald Sun*, 23/9/2007. The *Herald Sun* is a popular Australian daily newspaper.

References

Barad, K. (2003) Posthumanist Performativity: Toward an understanding of how matter comes to matter, *Signs*, 8:3, pp. 801–831.

Beckett, D. & Hager, P. (2000) Making judgements as the Basis for Workplace Learning: Towards an epistemology of practice, *International Journal of Lifelong Education*, 19:4, pp. 300–311.

Bingham, N. & Hinchcliffe, S. (2007) Editorial—Reconstituting Natures: Articulating other modes of living together, *Geoforum*, 39:1, pp. 8387

Bowker, G. & Star, S. L. (1999) *Sorting Things Out: Classification and its consequences* (Cambridge, MA, MIT Press).

Carolan, M. (2004) Ontological Politics: Mapping a complex environmental problem, *Environmental Values*, 13, pp. 497–522.

Cooper, R. & Law, J. (1995) Organization: Distal and proximal views, in: S. Bacharach, P. Gagliardi & B. Mundell (eds), *Research in the Sociology of Organizations: Studies of organizations with European tradition*, 13 (Greenwich, CT, JAI Press), pp. 237–274.

Day, C. (2004) *A Passion for Teaching* (London, RoutlegeFarmer).

Eraut, M. (2000) Non-formal learning and Tacit Knowledge in Professional Work, *The British Journal of Educational Psychology*, 70, pp. 113–136.

Ewenstein, B. & Whyte, J. (2009) Knowledge Practices in Design: The role of visual representations as 'epistemic objects', *Organization Studies*, 30:1, pp. 7–30.

Gherardi, S. (2006) *Organizational Knowledge: The texture of workplace learning* (Oxford, Blackwell).

Hiebert, J., Gallimore, R. & Stigler, J. (2002) A Knowledge Base for the Teaching Profession: What would it look like and how can we get one?, *Educational Researcher*, 31:5, pp. 3–15.

Ingvarson, L. & Rowe, K. (2008) Conceptualising and Evaluating Teacher Quality: Substantive and methodological issues, *Australian Journal of Education*, 52:1, pp. 5–35.

Lather, P. (1991) *Getting Smart: Feminist research and pedagogy with/in the postmodern* (New York, Routledge).

Latour, B. (2005) *Reassembling the Social: An introduction to actor-network-theory* (Oxford, Oxford University Press).

Law, J. (1992) Notes on the Theory of the Actor-network: Ordering, strategy, and heterogeneity. *Systems Practice*, 5:4, pp. 379–393.

Law, J. (1994) *Organizing Modernity* (Oxford, Blackwell).

Law, J. (2002) *Aircraft Stories: Decentering the object in technoscience* (Durham, NC, Duke University Press).

Law, J. (2004) *After Method: Mess in social science research* (London, Routledge).

Law, J. (2007) Making a Mess with Method, in: W. Outhwaite & S. P. Turner (eds), *The Sage Handbook of Social Science Methodology* (Thousand Oaks, CA, Sage) pp. 595–606.

Law, J. (2008) On Sociology and STS, *The Sociological Review*, 56:4, pp. 623–649.

Law, J. (2009) Actor-network Theory and Material Semiotics, in: B. S. Turner (ed.), *The New Blackwell Companion to Social Theory* (Oxford, Wiley-Blackwell), pp. 141–158.

Law, J. & Hassard, J. (1999) *Actor Network Theory and After* (Oxford, Blackwell).

Law, J. & Mol, A. (2008) Globalisation in Practice: On the politics of boiling pigswill, *Geoforum*, 39:1, pp. 133–143.

Law, J. & Singleton, V. (2000) Performing Technology's Stories: On social constructivism, performance, and performativity, *Technology and Culture*, 41:4, pp. 765–775.

Law, J. & Singleton, V. (2005) Object Lessons, *Organization*, 12:3, pp. 31–355.

Massey, D. (1999) Issues and Debates, in: D. Massey, J. Allen & P. Sarre (eds), *Human Geography Today* (Cambridge, Polity Press) pp. 3–21.

Mol, A. (1999) Ontological Politics: A word and some questions, in: J. Law & J. Hassard (eds), *Actor-network Theory and After* (Oxford, Blackwell), pp. 74–89.

Mol, A. (2002) *The Body Multiple: Ontology in medical practice* (Durham, NC, Duke University Press).

Mol, A. & Law, J. (1994) Regions, Networks and Fluids: Anaemia and social topology, *Social Studies of Science*, 24, pp. 641–671.

Moser, I. (2008) Making Alzheimer's Disease Matter: Enacting, intefering and doing politics of nature, *Geoforum*, 39:1, pp. 98–110.

Munro, R. (1997) Ideas of Difference: stability, social spaces and labour of division, in: K. Hetherington & R. Munro (eds), *Ideas of Difference: social spaces and the labour of division* (Oxford, Blackwell), pp. 3–24.

Nicolini, D., Gherardi, S. & Yanow, D. (eds) (2003) *Knowing in Organizations: A practice-based approach* (Armonk, NY, M.E. Sharpe).

Oppenheim, R. (2007) Actor-network Theory and Anthropology after Science, Technology, and Society, *Anthropological Theory*, 7:4, pp. 471–493.

Pickering, A. (1995) *The Mangle of Practice: Time, agency, and science* (Chicago, The University of Chicago Press).

Popkewitz, T. (2004) Educational Standards: Mapping who we are and are to become, *The Journal of the Learning Sciences*, 13:2, pp. 243–256.

Sachs, J. (2005) Teacher Professional Standards: A policy strategy to control, regulate or enhance the teaching profession?, in: N. Bascia, A. Cumming, A. Datnow, K. Leithwood & D. Livingstone (eds), *International Handbook of Educational Policy* (Dordrecht, Springer), pp. 579–592.

Shapin, S. & Schaffer, S. (1985) *Leviathan and the Air-pump: Hobbes, Boyle, and the experimental life* (Princeton, NJ, Princeton University Press).

Suchman, L. (1987) *Plans and Situated Actions: The problem of human-machine communication* (Cambridge, Cambridge University Press).

Sykes, G. & Plastrik, P. (1993) *Standard Setting as Educational Reform* (Washington, DC, American Association of Colleges for Teachers of Education).

Teaching Australia (2007) *National Professional Standards for Advanced Teaching and School Leadership: A consultation paper* (Canberra, Teaching Australia).

Thrift, N. (2008) *Non-representational Theory: Space, politics, affect* (London, Routledge).

Turnbull, D. (1997) Reframing Science and other Local Knowledge Traditions, *Futures*, 29:6, pp. 551–562.

Verran, H. (1998) Re-imagining Land Ownership in Australia, *Postcolonial Studies*, 1:2, pp. 237–254.

Verran, H., Christie, M., Anbins-King, B., Weeren, T. V. & Yunupingu, W. (2007) Designing Digital Knowledge Management Tools with Aboriginal Australians, *Digital Creativity*, 18:3, pp. 129–142.

Whatmore, S. (2006) Materialist Returns: Practising cultural geography in and for a more-than-human world. *Cultural Geographies*, 13:4, pp. 600–609.

White, J., Ferguson, P., Hay, T., Dixon, M. & Moss, J. (2004) Ownership and Identity: Developing and implementing teacher professional standards in Australia [Electronic Version]. *Unicorn*. Available at: http://www.austcolled.com.au/index.php?option=com_content&task=view&id=2196&Itemid=547

Yinger, R. (1987) Learning the language of Practice, *Curriculum Inquiry*, 17, pp. 293–318.

Yinger, R. & Hendricks-Lee, M. (2000) The Language of Standards and Teacher Education Reform, *Educational Policy*, 14:1, pp. 94–106.

6

Reading Educational Reform with Actor-Network Theory: Fluid spaces, otherings, and ambivalences

Tara Fenwick

Introduction

A recent conference that gathered leading scholars across the social sciences, including education, declared a growing central interest in the analytic category of material practice: 'the move now is to explain the emergence and experience of things'.[1] In analysing educational reform processes, what insights may be yielded, and what challenges encountered, when we focus on *material* practices, the politics they produce, and how they are entwined with agendas for educational change? One theoretical approach or 'sensibility' to a socio-material analysis is offered by actor-network theory (ANT), which has proliferated in the broad field of organizational studies and organizational change since the 1980s. In its early and enthusiastic iterations, as later critics pointed out, ANT tended to focus on the most powerful actors, to imply that all phenomena could be folded into a network ontology, and to overlook the location and gaze of the ANT analysis itself. Certain analytic constructs that emerged from the fine-grained early-ANT studies (e.g. Latour, 1996) also tended to be taken up in ways that eventually became formulaic. Later, reflexive re-thinkings of ANT such as Law and Hassard's *Actor Network Theory and After* (1999) pointed to the flowering of what is sometimes referred to as 'after-ANT' approaches: a wide-ranging diffusion of rich analyses that continued to trace how things become enacted through messy linkages among human and non-human elements, and to explore networks within networks, but which also honour multiple ontologies, ambivalences, and modes of enactment. Given this wide diversity, and given analysts' own care to distance themselves from any identifiable ANT orthodoxy or method, it seems safest to refer to a reading inspired by ANT approaches as 'ANT-ish'—which is the cautious if perhaps inelegant signifier adopted here.

But aside from a few accounts of educational innovation and policy drawing upon ANT (Fenwick & Edwards, 2010), educational change literature in the main offers little uptake of ANT concepts and the wider diffusion of after-ANT questions about ontological politics, otherness and mobilities. Yet these ANT inquiries into material practice, with their network readings that radically reconfigure human/nonhuman

Researching Education Through Actor-Network Theory, First Edition. Edited by Tara Fenwick and Richard Edwards.
Chapters © 2012 The Authors. Book compilation © 2012 Philosophy of Education Society of Australasia.

interconnections, would appear to offer useful engagements for debates in educational reform.

This discussion works from ANT-ish (including ANT and 'after-ANT') concepts and two extended examples of educational reforms to address the question: What does a network analysis contribute to understanding educational reform efforts? And to turn this question on its head while remaining within ANT-ish logic of radical relationality, translation and sociomaterial hetereogeneity about which more will be said later, the discussion considers: What can be understood about educational reform by stepping *outside* a network analysis, which while important for illuminating certain dynamics, can become a singular and totalizing representation that obscures others? In other words, how might after-ANT readings of educational reform help us to appreciate the spaces or blanks *beyond* networks, the partial and ambivalent belongings, and the otherness that cannot/should not be colonized by a single (networked) account? The argument ensuing from these questions suggests not only that ANT-ish readings open helpful questions for researching educational reform, but also that an educational consideration suggests useful spaces for the ongoing development of material semiotics and other after-ANT explorations.

ANT, After-ANT, and Educational Reform

Educational reform projects typically are premised on a functional logic of implemen-tation and measurement—usually directed towards changing pedagogy and other school structures in ways that will increase student achievement. Thus it is also an expensive, politically visible and complex enterprise that can attract close scrutiny of the public and a range of suspicious engagements from educators and educational administrators. Before examining what ANT might offer, it is important to acknowledge the different kinds of questions attracting inquiry into educational reform. One kind are critical questions about hegemonic reform purposes, the warring interests, agendas and exclu-sions embodied in certain state-initiated reform efforts (Taylor, Neu and Peters, 2002), and the oppressive regulatory effects on life in schools and teaching-learning processes. While important, these tend to focus solely on the social rather than the sociomaterial, and are based on *a priori* assumptions about social structures and subject categories that ANT readings call into question. A second kind are questions around the processes themselves of educational reform: how does it work over time and place, how do different actors respond, what rhetorical and material struggles ensue, and what actually changes? Volumes of educational change literature have addressed this problem. Conceptions borrowed from organizational studies range from episodic event-oriented transformation to incremental process-based recursive change (Weick & Quinn, 1999). Reform pro-cesses range from various iterations of strategic planning (preliminary explicit goals, stages of planned implementation including management of resistance, evaluated out-comes) to epidemiological diffusion (innovation is dropped into the container of the environment and gradually spreads through incentives and social processes such as persuasion and knowledge-sharing). Selected notions of complexity theory such as emergence, self-organization, recursion and fluidity adapted for educational managers (e.g. Fullan, 1993) have attracted popular appeal. Related models of the 'professional learning community' (Du Four & Eaker, 1998) centre educational reform at the site of the teacher, framing teacher learning as the problem and conventional if ambiguously romantic ideals of knowledge sharing in 'community' as the solution.

But the difficulty with this problematization of change processes in an organization is its starting point of conceiving the classroom, school or school district as distinct homogeneous organizations, and furthermore, organizations that are essentially social. Thus the category of the 'thing' to be changed is established *a priori* as an entity, separate from the thing that is understood to carry within it the force for change. Furthermore, the emphasis on personal and social processes, as important as these appear to be in constituting the cultural, emotional, political and psychological relations at work in education, completely ignores the material presences that exert force and are entwined with what appears to be human intention, engagement, resistance and change. A second problem, elaborated by Nespor (2002), is the conception of an educational innovation as a seed that is dropped into the pre-existing context of the school or school district. This presents context as a container and innovation as an origin that will grow (to use an arborescent metaphor), spread (to suggest an amorphous diffusion process), or be 'rolled out' (to use common parlance suggesting flattening of school landscapes with a road grader).

What then escapes analysis in the container-seed conception is the actual forms and outcomes of struggle negotiated at each of the myriad nodes of the process—each interaction between human elements (desires, pedagogical knowledge, attachments, intentions, etc.) and objects (such as textbooks, lab equipment, assessment forms, policy statements, parent newsletters, databases). Furthermore the diverse ongoing work required to sustain or even to stabilize any new educational change is often overlooked. The conventional story is that after implementation—whether it is conceptualized as growth, spread or roll-out—there is institutionalization (Crossan *et al.*, 1999) or, alternatively, failure, and that appears to be the end of the reform tale.

In contrast, Nespor (2002) argues from an ANT-ish approach:

> The point is that we need to understand 'school change' as at least partly about the ways school practices are made mobile, and what and how they connect as they move. What are the structures of connections or linkages? What materials are they made of? How do things change as they move? How do connections change with this movement? (pp. 367–68)

Actor-network theory offers concepts that illuminate dynamics of educational reform often left aside by these more structural or socially-focused analyses—including how actors emerge within the play of heterogeneous linkages among humans and nonhumans, and how the different actors that appear are performed into being by these linkages. As Law (1992) explains:

> This, then, is the core of the actor-network approach: a concern with how actors and organizations mobilise, juxtapose and hold together the bits and pieces out of which they are composed; how they are sometimes able to prevent those bits and pieces from following their own inclinations and making off; and how they manage, as a result, to conceal for a time the process of

translation itself and so turn a network from a heterogeneous set of bits and pieces each with its own inclinations, into something that passes as a punctualised actor. (p. 386)

The naturalization of a notion called 'educational reform' can be traced as an actor that was built over time and is now held in place by other actors and chains of ongoing effort. Instead of containers, ANT works from network metaphors to envisage change processes, including what appears to be teacher development and student learning, as the building of networks through all of these linkages. The more extended the network—the more entities that become 'enrolled' into its links and 'translated' or transformed in ways that support its work—the more likely it is to endure over time and to extend across regions. ANT looks closely at the translation process, tracing how an entity, human or nonhuman, becomes selected, enticed, persuaded and partially or fully changed in ways that mobilize it to join the network's movements. Further, ANT examines the various network strategies through which this durability and mobility is achieved, always focusing attention on the tiny, often mundane exchanges going on within the complex commotion of materials and human action that we think of as educational life.

An ANT reading of educational reform offers useful concrete insights about what goes on in the dynamics of change. In the field of organization studies, ANT analyses of innovation and change processes have proliferated to trace failures, showing how networks have imploded or failed to enrol sufficient entities to survive (Latour, 1996; Czarniawska & Hernes, 2005), as well as to examine successes, showing how the networks of 'macro-actors'—large initiatives, associations, bodies of knowledge or practices—have expanded and thrived. After-ANT readings focus on the material practices that become enacted and distributed, but also on the otherings that occur: the fluid spaces and partial belongings that can comprise what appears to be a powerful network (Law, 1999). In education reform, ANT-ish inquiry might ask: How does a new state initiative seeking to generate 'school improvement' produce itself into a 'thing'? How does 'it' (or they, for 'it' may be multiple things) become enacted over time and across different regions? What diverse negotiations and responses are generated through material practices, and how do these affect its durability and force? What exactly becomes engaged and connected, what becomes excluded, and how do these involvements shift over time? Where and how does power accumulate through these negotiations?

Education change literature offers a few ANT-ish analyses that provide in-depth tracings of these dynamics often obscured in considering educational reform. In the sections that follow, specific examples of these analyses are offered to show the fecundity and flexibility of ANT readings in studying educational reform. First, the different ANT approaches to network readings are introduced in the context of education. Second, an extended example is described of a study of university reform using a basic ANT network reading. Third, the after-ANT considerations of such a reading are described in more detail. In the fourth and fifth sections, an example of a large provincial reform in public education is presented to show how both ANT and after-ANT readings can be employed to glimpse critical dynamics of the reform process in its many spaces and ambivalences.

Network Readings and Educational Reform

Jan Nespor (1994, 2002) was one of the first educational researchers to employ ANT-associated network readings to analyse educational processes and reforms. In doing so, Nespor carefully distinguishes this approach from that of social network analysis, which treats actors as well-defined entities pre-existing their social relations, and network ties as static and neutral. Instead, Nespor treats networks as assemblages of heterogeneous entities such as written curricula, videos, human actions and buildings that can move educational practices across space and time (2002 p. 369). Entities themselves are neither solid objects and subjects nor clearly separated from their context. They are each an effect produced through a set of relations that is constantly in motion. The network that appears through the linkages among these entities is a trace, reasonably stable, of a series of translations that have changed and continue to change each entity participating within the network. In fact, network effects work on and are exercised by entities that may not be enrolled into a particular network.

However in education, Nespor (1994) argues that ANT's tendency to focus on powerful central actors does not particularly improve understandings of those at the margins—most obviously and importantly, students—whose identity and action is tied up with being mobilized. Furthermore, if ANT readings focus on a network's centre, the observer might be captured by the appearance of flow from every direction which misses the entrenchments and stable divisions that are more visible 'from a distance'. In education, these 'deeply worn channels' (1994, p. 15) formed by particularly durable networks such as racism and colonialism—not to be confused with anterior conceptions of 'social structures'—are critically important to analysis. But far from abandoning ANT for education, Nespor (1994) concludes that its frames help illuminate the 'structure of networks, the ties that bind them, and the nature of whatever it is that flows through them' (p. 23). Furthermore, ANT readings can show precisely how educational innovations and practices order space and time as well as forms of participation in networks of power. That is, ANT penetrates the different sociomaterial negotiations occurring in the evolution, extension and sedimentation of these networks that appear to discipline people and knowledge as well as technology and the natural world so effectively.

Important critiques of the network metaphor (Bloomfield & Vurdubakis 1999; Hassard, Law & Lee 1999; Lee & Brown 1994) have pointed out that it appears to totalize reality, implying that all possible elements, entities and imminences are accounted for and securely positioned within network(s). Annemarie Mol and John Law (1994) are among those who have conceptualized other ontologies alongside networks, such as fluid regions or ambiguous, emergent spaces and relations. One can imagine multiple network forms and intensities whose very multiplicity of shifting interactions creates fluid improvisational spaces. Despite some unfortunate metaphorical baggage of networks as self-contained linear pipelines or reified engineered linkages, networks can be envisioned as far more ephemeral and rhizomatic in nature. Networks are simply webs that grow through connections. The connections can be thick and thin, rigid and limp, close and distant, dyadic and multiple, material and immaterial. And the connections have spaces between them. Barbara Czarniawska and Tor Hernes (2005) propose that we think of action nets rather than networks to avoid the sense of inevitability and lock-down that 'network' seems to imply for some. But for the purposes of this discussion, the word 'network' will be used. This is intended to invoke the simple but plastic concept of an unspecified set of connected points or nodes with un-represented spaces among them. The word also serves as a useful reminder both of the precariousness and unpredictability of any network's formation and continuity, as well as the multiple shapes and lengths it can assume—from a large open fishing net to a tightly clasped net bag, from a sticky and multi-netted local web to a far-reaching network gathering global industries into some standardized practice.

In terms of educational reform, Nespor (2002) argues that a network reading shifts the tendency to view certain participants as 'reformers' and others as 'contexts', to understanding that all are part of materially heterogeneous networks that have unfolded geographically and historically and that overlap and relate with one another. Reforms and contexts mutually create one another. Reforms are 'contingent *effects* of struggles and negotiations in which groups try to define themselves and their interests by linking up with other relatively durable and extensive networks' (Nespor, 2002, p. 366). Elements that appear to lie outside a school's networked activity, such as a parent for example, are in fact connected to and partly produced by it. For example, Nespor shows how the school's network of reform extends into a parent's actions and identity through a child's homework. The homework was treated by the parent not just as an object of performance circulating within the school, but also as a comparator to the child's homework produced years earlier. Then this representation was 'hybridized' with terms of the national curricula debates, which 're-territorialized the homework' and re-scaled the local school into part of the national problem, while translating national-level debates into specific critiques of the local school reform. The mother doesn't just participate in the school reform but actively reframes it into terms that she can oppose. For Nespor, the important questions for educational reform that can be illuminated through such network readings include 'how and in what forms people, representations and artifacts move, how they are combined, where they get accumulated, and what happens when they are hooked up with other networks already in motion' (p. 376).

A First Reading of Reform: Extending the Network

One study that explores these questions in educational change using an early ANT concept will be described in some detail to show more precisely what a network reading might reveal. Jo Ann Luck (2008) examined the processes of implementing a video-conferencing system in an educational institution, Central Queensland University in Australia (CQU). Working with Callon's (1986) original 'moments of translation' (problematization, interessement, enrolment and mobilization), and treading carefully to avoid reifying a particular analytic model and colonizing the reform landscapes to fits its precepts, Luck offers useful insights about the ways in which a new network of usage grows. She traces how the network moves in education among highly diverse groups of actors—faculties, support staff, facilities and students—distributed across diverse regional sites and already enrolled in durable networks of teaching-learning practices. This analysis is particularly useful for, as Busch (1997) has argued, university knowledge disciplines and practices are heavily 'blackboxed' and particularly resistant to new translations. Using an ANT analysis, Busch argued that universities consist of highly durable actor-networks held in place by linkages among vast networks of equipment, architectures, other institutions, and historical relational patterns.

The CQU reform process began with certain activities at the university level (video-conferencing trials, forming a steering group, writing a grant) that created loose local networks. These local networks aligned with national networks pressuring for reduced spending, increased student access and a unified national system in higher education in ways that not only granted these more distant networks material presence and strength in the university, but helped to strengthen the local networks. Luck also shows the importance, perhaps particularly in hierarchical institutions such as higher education, of a 'heterogeneous engineer' who exerts sufficient authority to define the 'problem' in ways that other actors will accept. In the CQU case, Luck presents the university's senior management as this engineer. However, a simple decree from managers rarely accomplishes implementation. In this case, a 'Future Directions' document circulated by senior management problematized existing teaching-learning systems and convincingly linked these with the funding and viability problems of the institution. This document became a key intermediary—an actor that can translate thinking and behaviour—in the form of an 'immutable mobile', an inscription that itself represents a translation of a series of events and actors and that has achieved sufficient durability to circulate across far-reaching space-times.

This document combined with various objects to problematize existing practice and begin a process that Callon called 'interessement'—where one actor, human or nonhuman, influences and attempts to join with another in order to enrol its participation in a new network. These objects included, for example:

- a logo—'Vision 97' for the initiative;
- grants made available to install the new interactive video-communication (IVC) systems in classrooms;
- letters sent to students and parents guaranteeing that they could complete a degree at home and avoid relocation costs;
- prospective promotions for support staff involved in implementation, and;
- demonstrations of the higher quality and convenience of the proposed IVC systems comparative to existing temporary cabinets rolled from room to room.

As Luck notes, once there are rooms, screens, wires, microphones, policies and training schemes in place, '[the IVC implementation] is more credible and compelling as a useful system for performing teaching activities' (p. 181). The active circulation of these objects throughout CQU's distributed sites occurred not only through mail, media and announcements, but also through establishment of a 'walking group'. This group visited all constituents in all regional campuses to engage them directly in the initiative, talking about and touching components of the IVC. Luck's analysis shows how what goes on at these different nodes of circulating objects and humans—the attempts to translate through problematizing, persuading and enrolling at the far-flung edges of the network's potential reach—actually builds the new network of practice bit by bit.

Actors' enrolment in the network is, however, precarious, and needs to be stabilized if the network is to endure. Luck shows the multiple negotiations that continued to occur throughout the network to inscribe the various actors into certain roles that became glued together in a configuration that could perform the new IVC teaching-learning system. Much of this negotiation was at the linkages of objects and technologies with human intentions, expectations, and attempted actions. Each of these linkages embedded endless numbers of artefacts, mediators, and inscriptions negotiating connections that gradually became locked into the new network. For example, sound issues of the new system entailed speakers and speaker adjustments, recordings, variable control panels, refinements to microphone size and links to manage the unique classroom demands on the IVC, carpet installation to address noise concerns, technicians, designers, trials, written concerns about cost escalations, and so forth.

Luck's study in effect traces the various forms of ordering that can hold precarious relationship in place, as described by Law (2003). Durability, which is ordering through time, can be achieved by 'delegation' to the most durable materials that can maintain their relational patterns, and to other networks to hold in place these durable materials (technicians and repair agencies hold microphones in place). Mobility, which is ordering through space, can be achieved through what Latour called 'immutable mobiles' that travel, binding various locales into central modes of calculation. Centres of calculation and translation order direction, voice and representation, often by anticipating the responses and reactions of the materials to be translated. And finally the scope of ordering is extended when strategies of translation are reproduced in a range of network locations.

Overall Luck's network reading helps illustrate how, in educational initiatives of innovation and reform, insufficient attention is often granted to the active role of objects and technology. These tend to be treated as brute things to be installed rather than dynamic actors. To grow a network, relationships need to be built carefully and flexibly among the mix of objects-technologies-humans, attuning to nonhuman actors' capacity to act back in ways that network engineers may not have anticipated. Luck points out various strategies through which a fragile new network of these relationships is extended and strengthened in a successful educational reform. For example, 'key' actors are employed as intermediaries, as many actors are added as possible, and alignments are made with other, distal networks such as national priorities and international discourses in education. Such strategies contribute to the extension, durability and even irreversibility of a new network, with perhaps undesired forms of entrenchment. But the network is also experiencing continual challenges and shifts at its multiple micro-connections as actors discover and exploit weaknesses in inscriptions, or enact 'anti-programs'. Constant attunement to these shifts and flexible adjustment is the essential everyday work of those actors interested in sustaining a network of educational reform. The work is ongoing not only at these nodes but also in the overall shape of the educational institution as the new networks stretch and translate its appearance, its functions, and its extensions into spaces that appear to lie beyond it.

Re-thinking the Reading: Centrality and Otherness

Luck's (2008) analysis of educational reform employs an early-ANT model to trace the ongoing, unpredictable, often difficult socio-material transactions at a micro-level. While useful, this model is not without its critics who have pointed out several cautions for researchers. One is the tendency for any theoretical approach like this to become sedimented into an explanatory frame that is imposed, *a priori*, on the data. This is especially problematic for ANT, which has striven to maintain a fluid, decentred and exploratory approach that challenges *a priori* concepts and structures and honours complexities of immanent, emergent phenomena. However in response, McLean and Hassard (2004) argue that the four-stage model can be viewed more as a heuristic or 'sensitizing' concept adapted to make sense of complex observations. Analysts of educational reform need not slavishly impose four steps and expect a linear process, but appreciate that translation is ongoing, iterative and disorderly.

Two further critiques of 'early-ANT' applied to educational reform involve the problems of centrality or focus on 'big actors', and the problem of difference or otherness. The issue of centrality emerged when so many ANT studies focused on the development of large, powerful networks such as major policy initiatives. While ANT concepts are clearly helpful in illuminating the movements resulting in success—or failure, depending on the perspective and interests of those judging—of a major reform, the danger is lack of reflexivity about what the analyst is including and excluding. As Strathern (1996) points out, the ANT decision to 'cut the network', to establish boundaries around the object of inquiry, is problematic if it simply adopts the categories of its subjects and focus on what appears to be most important and visible. This was Nespor's (1994) difficulty with ANT applied to education in ways that focused on big projects and ignored those with less visibility, fewer strategies or complex relations to networks. This issue opens out to a whole series of questions about otherness in ANT, which Hetherington and Law (2000) summarized in a special journal issue devoted to the topic. They argued that the metaphor of the network can presume to colonize all dimensions, elements, layers and spaces of a phenomenon, as though everything that exists is drawn somewhere, somehow, into the relentless knots of networks extending infinitely. A network reading potentially 'leaves no room for alterity and allows for nothing to stand outside the relations that it orders through its descriptions of the word' (Hetherington & Law, 2000, p. 128). This problem extends further than colonizing or 'speaking for' not only marginalized humans but also marginalized objects. The problem is also about dividing space and action according to issues of relation and difference: what becomes connected and mobilized into a network and what remains different according to that network's terms and relations. What of alterity that is blank, unexpected, novel and ambivalent? What of otherness that lies within or flows across network alignments, that is incoherent or non-representable? These questions warn the ANT-reading from presuming to offer any single account of events, and alert attention to spaces and discontinuities that may be distorted through a conventional network reading.

However, as Julia Clarke (2002) has argued in her analysis of a major literacy policy initiative in the UK, education continues to struggle with 'big actor' reforms that do threaten to enrol wider constituents, including critically challenging actors and counter-networks of resistance, sedimenting all of these heterogeneous elements into powerful networks that can function oppressively. ANT analysis is particularly useful in tracing these power relations, showing how connections and translations among materials as well as language and social processes can appear to lock hegemonies into place. Clearly

ANT-readings need to move as carefully and reflexively as possible, mindful of their own tendency to create obligatory points of passage, cautious in neither totalizing nor ignoring phenomena unfolding, and mindful of both their own highly provisional accounts and the entanglement of these accounts in constituting the phenomena being read. But limitations of gaze, as in all forms of research, are matters of caveat, not censure for a particular theoretical approach such as ANT.

A Second Reading: Mobilizing and Sustaining Reform

Let us consider another example of an educational reform launched in 2000 in Alberta, Canada and still thriving, rather astonishingly given some of its precepts, at the time of writing 9 years later. Why? How? In the following ANT-ish reading, based on reports of the project rather than empirical tracings,[2] certain concepts appear useful to go some way to address these questions. ANT helps illuminate moments in the enrolment and translation of actors, the importance of particular mobile inscriptions that travel about ordering particular activities, the problematization and relations that establish centres of calculation and translation, and the overall gradual assemblage and strengthening of a network through various strategies. But the case also resists an overly tight emphasis on network-building, for non-networkable spaces and otherness can be glimpsed when we probe what is going on in the unfoldings of this network. Indeed, certain otherings appear in some ways to be enabling the most visible network to proceed with its work.

The following account is not intended to collapse this complexity into a glib performance of (otherness-enriched) network reading, but to suggest the potential for ANT-ish approaches to not only analyse how powerful networks become set in motion through educational reform but also to gesture towards gaps and more fluid spaces within and among these networks. The case is an educational reform called the 'Alberta Initiative for School Improvement' (AISI) that states its official goal as being 'to improve student learning and performance by fostering initiatives that reflect the unique needs and circumstances of each school authority' (Alberta Learning, 1999, p. 4). The initiative has made available Alberta government funds to any school or school district whose proposal for a 3-year school improvement project is judged by the provincial ministry, Alberta Education, to be acceptable according to clearly communicated criteria—particularly the criterion to improve student achievement, mostly through measurement on provincial standardized tests.[3] The first 3-year AISI period or 'cycle' supposedly showed such general success in improving student test scores and meeting individual projects' student achievement targets, according to government reports (Alberta Learning, 2004), that AISI was renewed for two more 3-year cycles since start-up.

The initiative is characterized by several features that are surprising in a context where bitter disputes between the government, school districts and teachers marked the 6 years of educational restructuring for accountability prior to 2000 (Taylor *et al.*, 2002), when districts were amalgamated, standardized student testing expanded, and business planning introduced in a 'wave of top-down, seemingly ideologically driven package of educational reforms' (Burger *et al.*, 2001, para 12). Perhaps the most surprising feature is the vast number of schools and districts that became involved and continued their involvement in the AISI reform, despite the recent history of stormy relations. A second point of interest is that AISI established a partnership of the government with all educational professional associations, an alliance whose sustainability over 9 years is worth noting given the rather wide range of ideology and interests represented by these organizations.[4] Third, the government has committed more funds to AISI than to any other educational reform and further, in an historically unusual arrangement, grants these funds directly to school districts. Approximately $500 million CAD to date has been committed to fund projects in about 1600 schools (of Alberta's 2246 total number of schools) (McEwan, 2008). Finally, AISI has managed to actively involve university faculties of education in its projects, despite broad areas where philosophical contestation and resistance might normally be expected. For example, the current AISI website, an exhaustive collection of individual project reports, province-wide meta-analyses and AISI histories, databases of 'lessons learned' in every curricular area etc., liberally foregrounds concepts such as 'evidence-based' education, universalized 'best practices' of pedagogy, and classroom-based research limited to improving teacher techniques towards outcomes-based student achievement.

So the question of how AISI managed to extend as far as it did, enrolling and sustaining participation among such diverse constituents, is of particular interest. A network reading could show the importance of intermediaries, like money, in attracting participants. Superintendents for example, after a decade of funding cutbacks and restructuring, were highly motivated by the offer of cash for improvement proposals even when they were aware of their own 'translation' in accepting the grants. One superintendent explained:

> The name of the game is conditional granting. They call it enveloping or whatever terminology you want, but it works ... because it creates the behaviour you want. In my instance for example, AISI [Alberta Initiative for School Improvement] money, politically I can't afford to let over a million dollars go. I would get crucified ... by my board, by our parents, because we let a million dollars slide. They don't care what has to happen to make it happen, just get it for us ... . They say we want you to jump one foot and it works because the carrot is one foot off the ground. (Taylor *et al.*, 2002, p. 476)

The attraction for teachers lay at least partly in the apparently open nature of AISI projects. The project problem, content and methods are left entirely to the discretion of the school or district applicant—as long as they can demonstrate an improvement to student achievement. Most early projects were oriented to improving student literacy and mathematics achievement. Other popular areas emerging over the nine years were developing pedagogies for English-as-Second-Language instruction, for integrating technology into classrooms and for 'differentiated instruction' (instructional approaches to meet different student special needs and learning styles). In all of these projects, a stream of new materials came rolling into classrooms: class sets of mathematics puzzles and blocks, new computers and teaching software, textbooks and teacher guides. Teachers were intimately enmeshed in putting to work not only these student materials, but also the new instruments of data collection that each project needed to design.

Once districts and teachers were mobilized to design and apply for projects for which they had local affection and commitment, intermediaries began to circulate around the province that helped translate these energies into certain consistent practices. The project proposals, for example, demanded structures of pre-and post-project measurement of student performance, as well as a research design. Each project also was required to produce an annual report according to a template created by the government AISI office, a report that focused attention on technical information such as improvement objectives, key strategies, evaluation methods, student outcomes, effective practices, sustainability, what worked and what didn't work, etc. (Alberta Education, 2008), with little space for exploring or recognizing complexity. These reports are all posted publicly on a searchable web-based database, an inscription which collapses, orders and translates complex multiplicity into one centre of calculation. Other centers draw together the nodes of the projects to further reinforce the network. A province-wide AISI conference sponsored annually by the province features presentations from teachers leading the projects. AISI coordinators, known as 'lead' teachers with credibility in their district, are trained for the role and gathered together throughout the year for support. Now appointed in 74% of Alberta districts, these individuals represent more intense nodes of translation spreading throughout the extending network.

The concept of 'translation' in large-scale reform implementation reaches beyond the conventional considerations of change theory for actors' personal attitudes or levels of adoption, their social ability to interpret and integrate (Crossan *et al.*, 1999), or their capacity to shift institutional structures. Translation examines how, in the process of implementation, relationships with things actually become transmuted. Textbooks and plastic blocks and computer games became objects of study. Lesson plans became experiments. Everyday interactions with students became 'benchmarking'. Student assignments became AISI findings. In other words, the translation of teacher to (AISI) researcher fundamentally changes the pedagogic gaze, identity, and relationships.

As all of these practitioners struggled to develop project proposals and final reports, indeed to reconceptualize classroom work as an AISI project, the province's six universities were mobilized to assist schools with meeting the research requirements. Each was allotted sufficient funds to appoint its own AISI coordinator and office, which began generating websites about classroom research methods and distributing materials such as measurement tools in workshops and school visits to show teachers how to collect and analyze their own data, 'benchmark' student achievement, etc. In each of these moves, an ANT-reading of available documents illuminates how the reform spread not through top-down imposition but through circulation—of inscriptions, intermediaries, collaborations with objects and technologies, and a host of actors translating one another, assembling highly heterogeneous institutions, political interests, philosophies of knowledge and suspicions about reform.

A network is strengthened when it becomes linked with other existing actor-networks. In the AISI case, other networks besides the universities became hooked in. The provincial teachers' association viewed AISI projects as sites for professional learning communities (PLC), and actively promoted both the AISI Clearinghouse of project reports and lessons learned, and PLC workshops to support AISI projects (Alberta Teachers' Association, 2008).

Clearly AISI appears to have established and extend itself as a far-reaching and durable network. It has mobilized hundreds of teachers and administrators (linked with classroom materials, databases, school timetables and equipment)—as well as universities and professional associations—to accept their own translation into designated roles that extended and stabilized the network. AISI seems to work partly as a mediation between the local networks of schools and districts, and the more extended but distinct networks of the teachers' association, the university's education teaching and research programs, and the government network. Each network maintained its own life and circulations while being bound up, for different reasons and to support different agendas, in the circulating inscriptions and translations of the AISI network. The government coordinator of AISI activities claims that 'multiple sources of evidence' show that AISI has had 'profound effect on education in Alberta' particularly in 'improved student learning, renewed focus on teaching and learning, better decision-making based on evidence, job-embedded professional development, and shared and distributed leadership' (McEwan, 2008, p. 6).

Re-reading Reform: Fluid Spaces and Ambivalent Belongings

However there is much that is obscured by this reading focused on centricity, on how the reform extended and stabilized itself. What beckons some acknowledgment, at least, are the spaces and the otherness shadowed away by the foregrounding of a seemingly immutable 'AISI network' as though it were cut into the province like a madly branching river. Different spaces, even different forms of space, can be discerned moving in and around the most visible network of power. Further, there seem to be different forms of belonging to this network and its tributaries. The simple question of how translation occurs does not reach far enough. What about partial translations—when and why do these occur, and how do the resulting ambivalent belongings affect the overall network?

Returning to the teachers who appeared to become so widely engaged in the projects, it might be understandable that these in fact represented a rather open space. While the start and end points were shaped by the prescribed proposal and report templates, and while the objective was pre-determined to be student achievement, the freedom to choose the content, activities and materials for the project opened an important space of local innovation and control. In other words, projects were widely diverse in their question as well as their pedagogical content. Some schools worked with the prescribed provincial curricula, and others focused on implementing what might be considered more popular (perhaps even theoretically questionable) initiatives such as 'multiple intelligences'. Teachers try new pedagogical practices, collect data in the classroom evidencing the success of these practices, and report results. The projects are referred to as action research (Parsons *et al.*, 2006), and appear to offer opportunities for teachers to engage creatively in generating and legitimating the classroom-oriented, practice-based knowledge that advocates of teacher research have been promoting in recent decades (e.g. Cochran-Smith & Lytle, 1999). Teachers were invited by AISI to become translated into knowledge producers and authorities. In fact the university representatives were translated by AISI into roles that served, rather than disseminated, knowledge production. These local spaces of innovation and discretionary action are critical, argue

Bowker and Star (2000), to maintain network extension by retaining 'intimacy in its detailed knowledge of the nuances of practice' (p. 232). Too much standardized control and network imperative threatens its manageability and survival.

These spaces might be seen as the gaps between the network knots, if the knots are simply the visible parts of the project—the required reports—that are calculated and gathered into dense sites. But like a fishnet, big spaces can open where these calculations do not specify type of pedagogies, direction of project, pace of implementation, enrolment of actors, standard instruments or texts, etc. Since the scrutiny of the text focuses most on the measurable student achievement, these spaces exist as an unrepresented other to the network. The actual materials used, the pedagogical approaches tried, the various experiments and failures and upsets, the everyday commotion of classroom action, the wide uses of objects—all of this swirls in a space outside the attention of the network. This other is assumed to be present by the network's reports, but is in fact absent. It escapes representation in an otherness that Law terms 'manifest absence' (Law, 2004, xx). Thus, what constitutes an AISI project, the thing that is linked into such an apparently durable network, exists in different dimensions. It exists as the neatly ordered project reports and all the meta-analyses generated by these. It exists as the funded set of materials and activities that teachers and administrators manage and plan. But the AISI project, unbounded, is also the immanent, ineffable events of the classroom reality, which as Thrift (2000) argues, always and necessarily lives outside network space. Perhaps the only central thing holding together the AISI network is the circulating insistence on increasing measurable student achievement. But even this notion appears to slide in the messy spaces of the network. Stelmach (2004) for example, shows that at the level of parent and teacher discussions, impact on achievement was often overlooked: AISI project success was explained in rather symbolic terms, and a perception existed that as long as strategies that were implemented during the project had life beyond the 3-year project, AISI had succeeded.

For the universities the AISI projects exist as a research enterprise. But fluid spaces open here, too. Approvals for ethical research procedures, for instance, which the university regards as essential in any project that collects and represents data, fell into a space between direct grants from government to schools and university assistance to conduct research (Parsons *et al.*, 2006). Teacher-researcher training, normally conducted by the faculties of education through accredited courses and programs under their control, now was permitted, indeed encouraged, in spaces with no tuition, progression or clear disciplinary authority. In network logic, university personnel were simply enrolled into extensions of knowledge exchange reaching beyond the districts. But in fact, these extensions created fissures that generated complicated spaces where various dimensions had to be negotiated.

These spaces of manifest absence are not concretely visible to AISI's continual translations, although their presence can be circumscribed as inside or outside the network. However beyond these spaces lie other regions, or perhaps other forms of spaces, that a strict network reading of the massive AISI reform and its intersecting networks cannot circumscribe. One of the most obvious of these is the othering of inquiry that reaches outside the a-critical and a-political AISI circumscription of particular forms and questions of research. Everything in AISI is, after all, geared to improving instructional methods for a narrow set of academic student engagements. Only rare projects address students' experiences beyond these engagements, or analyse issues of equity and justice. Few projects explored poverty or health, racism, homophobia, religious discrimination or social exclusion in schools despite the prominence of these issues in the education system. None critically examined educational policy, or analysed systemic politics and power relations in school practices, texts, relations, and so forth. Utterly absent was educational research reflecting post-structuralist, feminist, post-colonialist, or any number of other contemporary and increasingly widespread orientations in university-based educational research. In fact, in one presentation to the Alberta school superintendents association, AISI was claimed to be the 'gold standard' of improvement models that sends a 'clear message' to universities that the only valid research is that which reflects student achievement results (Reeves, 2005, p. 15).

However with the universities enrolled in extending and strengthening the AISI network, the appearance is created of scholarly approval and support for the AISI-endorsed form of educational research: that is, research that focuses on measurable improvement to teaching methods to produce measurable improvement in student test scores with no attention to social relations, power and positionality, cultural difference, inequitable structures, systemic problems, undecidability, contradiction or messiness— all the dimensions of critical inquiry that academic educational research has been leading. Further, 'action research' becomes converted to solving pre-determined problems, an AISI formulation that completely ignored Alberta scholars' explorations of classroom action research as participatory, hermeneutic, emancipatory, and emergent (e.g. Carson & Sumara, 1997). But were the universities truly enrolled? When we examine their actual involvement, it appears that each of the province's six universities had simply used AISI funds to cover partial salary of one faculty member designated as an AISI coordinator and provide some clerical support. Some, but certainly not all, of these university-based AISI offices became active in training teachers and school district AISI coordinators in research methods, and maintaining websites to support AISI research (Parsons *et al.*, 2006). But AISI activity and offices do not appear on the university websites. And surprisingly, given the rich abundance of AISI-sponsored classroom research proceeding around the province, almost no faculty research has been conducted around any aspect of AISI—not even critical analyses, and very few graduate theses. There may be diverse reasons for this indifference—perhaps faculty scholars are deliberately distancing their work from AISI-prescribed projects, or expressing distaste for classroom research and teachers as researchers, or are simply unaware of the possibilities or too busy with competing priorities. Whatever the reasons, the six university faculties of educational research can be described as belonging to the AISI network only as ambivalent members. They have accepted the funds and the attached responsibilities to promote AISI, they have maintained their names as full partners on the AISI website, but the translation of their roles has remained minimal.

Parents, too, were enrolled in ambivalent ways in the AISI network. While AISI projects required active involvement of 'parents and the community to work collaboratively to introduce innovative and creative initiatives' based upon local needs and circumstances (Alberta Learning, 1999), there was general agreement that parent engagement in AISI projects was peripheral, relegated to receiving special newsletters about AISI project activities and attending show-and-tell events. Perhaps not surprisingly, the general amount and nature of integrative parent involvement in schools remained largely unaffected by AISI (Parsons *et al.*, 2006). One study of this phenomenon (Stelmach, 2004) described a school district that installed a special 'Action Team' to mobilize parents in AISI participation, by creating home-school linkages and active parental engagement in project strategies to improve learning. However the Action Team's discussions were kept separate from the teachers' curriculum meetings, and parents felt they were interfering inappropriately both with teachers' time and teachers' legitimate authority over classroom decisions.

> As one parent suggested, 'I felt that we as parents didn't have as much to offer because, first of all we had to learn what the issues were.' When teachers came up with ideas, this parent admitted that the others on the Action Team agreed to go along with the teachers because parents and community members felt ill equipped to offer alternatives. In doing this, parents affirmed the cultural expectation that teachers are responsible for student learning. (Stelmach, 2004, para 34)

The translation of parents was limited to highly circumscribed roles in the network: receiving personal invitations to student award ceremonies and special newsletters about AISI progress, attending designated parent lunches and the like. Issues of persistent parental marginalization through social class, racialization and culture are not even recognized. Still, some parents participated, even in the awkward dialogues inviting parent suggestions that they sensed were unwelcome. Meanwhile, as Stelmach (2004) notes, the school entrance sign continued to regulate all visitors to report to the office, announcing clear insider-outsider boundaries and control of territory. Despite parents' apparent inscription as network participants in various AISI texts and attendances, they remained actors at the edges. Their partial translation recalls Nespor's (1994) warning about ANT's presumption of ever-expanding fluid networks: the social world of schools flows in very deep channels.

  What of the translation of teachers into actors in the AISI-network? According to a government AISI report, teachers have not only been converted into successful AISI researchers, but also into continuous learners focused on 'what works' orientation. In other words, the complex space and pedagogic flows comprising what it is to be a 'teacher' has been converted into measures of teaching capacity based on application of evidence-based practice: 'Teachers now view themselves as learners and engage in inquiry related to the impact of their practices on student learning. They talk about gathering evidence of effective practices and use it to determine what works and what doesn't work for students' (Alberta Learning, 2004, p. 48). However, in one of the only studies available that actually followed the actors in AISI, a more complex picture emerges. Mary-Lee Judah and George Richardson (2006) show how teachers they interviewed were both excited by the opportunity afforded by AISI to creatively develop new knowledge with their students and colleagues, and dismayed by the regulatory strictures and mandated involvement of the projects. In other words, teachers were 'caught between competing discourses of personal empowerment and individual autonomy on the one hand and of the need to respond to externally driven measures of accountability and excellence on the other' (Judah & Richardson, 2006, p. 69). Teachers who were AISI coordinators, the study showed, also struggled in imposing projects on their colleagues that seemed to be highly regulated yet that offered potentially rich opportunity and time for professional learning.

Time itself became another space of complex enrolment. As AISI offered sufficient funds for substitutes to release teachers from classroom time, schools and districts could enable teacher gatherings for building curriculum and learning new strategy. For teachers, claim Parsons *et al.* (2006), this was an especially welcome space for new emergences. However, time away from the class occasion is not release from the class activity, as all teachers know who have labored late nights over substitute lesson plans for the next day of their absence. In AISI as with many educational implementations, teachers must maintain simultaneous presence in different forms and in different spaces that are not all delineated by the terms of the powerful network. Teachers inhabit life in their AISI enrolment as both researchers and as learners of teaching practice, in their ongoing classroom responsibilities as immanent engagement in that practice, in their regulated accounting to the government, and in their defense of boundaries defining their knowledge authority and practice—boundaries which AISI network strategies cannot re-inscribe and re-order despite continuing struggle so to do.

Not surprisingly, translation in educational reforms such as AISI is partial and diverse, representing ambivalent belongings rather than transformation and fluid spaces that escape network representation. Still, they are belongings, and the powerful AISI network in Alberta, like the IVC network in Central Queensland, has become durable as an extended set of connections among highly heterogeneous entities. Within and among these connections, however, are multiple openings and ungoverned regions where local, creative and unpredictable activity and identities can play.

Conclusion

Actor-network theory, as a diffuse array of analytic approaches, is argued here to afford fruitful questions for considering educational reform. In its conceptions of translations that link together heterogeneous materials, knowledges, emotions, agencies, bodies and technologies, ANT examines the micro-negotiations at these different links. It examines the ongoing work to enrol and mobilize all of these human and nonhuman elements into common practices and understandings that begin to resemble a stabilized 'network' of educational reform. In this sensibility, ANT readings ask, just how did this network come to extend itself? How did these varied entities come to be combined? What occurred at the various nodes and linkages to connect them? What kinds of connections are continuing to hold, why, and what else is working to hold them in place? What changes occurred in the process of these connections—and what didn't change? Where did resistance emerge and what happened to it? But beyond these questions are others, inspired by after-ANT readings (e.g. Law & Hassard, 1999). These questions strive to de-centre ANT's tendency to centrist, colonized network readings of all reality, and recall the otherness that happily escapes such obsessive tracing.

In terms of educational reform, the early kind of ANT analysis is useful to reveal the material interactions through which a major change initiative is successfully mobilized—even one that might be expected to inspire widespread critique and collective resistance among educators, such as mandated action research to create and measure evidence-based practice. The approach of tracing the moments of translation and strategies of ordering practices and identities helps illuminate how the change, conceptualized as a growing network, gradually extends and becomes durable. In effect, the network inscribes a new geography of social and material relations throughout an educational system. This analysis is particularly useful in tracing how ideas, practices and new technologies that appear to be completely foreign and irreconcilable with existing networks can eventually insinuate themselves as the new norms. This analysis can also examine the myriad wider connections implicated in educational reform. As Nespor (2002) asks, when the meanings of schools are connected to all sorts of things outside the border of the school, should not school change efforts address these relations?

However within this reading, we can see how translations vary: some entities are more peripherally enrolled, and some translations hold but are very leaky. The linkages often create ambivalent belongings, where people, things and collectives struggle to protect practices from inscription through these new connections at the same time as they work the connections for their own purposes. And we also see the other spaces that are non-calculable, and in fact not even representable by network logic. In the AISI network, local spaces allowed district and classroom project invention in directions that the network did not attempt to order—beyond allocating the space of design. These can be characterized as spaces within the network, held loosely between the ordering nodes. But other spaces also float alongside the network, unrecognized, uncaptured and unrelated to both its ordering processes and to the ANT researcher's network logic. These are the spaces of both ambivalence and of contradiction, where the direction and nature of action is undecidable and unpredictable. In these spaces, creative possibilities can emerge. However, they also can be contained and obscured through network strategies to block counter networks of invention.

The ANT-ish readings suggested here not only trace the most visible movements of ordering in educational reforms, but also gesture to the more elusive, more messy, more promising otherness of new possibilities. That is, attention to the socio-material connections and their patterns can discern not only closures but also openings in mass reform efforts, spaces for flux and instability embedded within and floating apart from the network. Most important, such readings can open inquiry into processes through which such possibilities can be protected and amplified, recognized, and perhaps connected together, where appropriate, to realize alternative educational change.

Notes

1. *Materialising the Subject: phenomenological and post-ANT objects in the social sciences*, University of Manchester, 26–27 Feb 2009. Available at: http://www.cresc.ac.uk/events/forum/MaterialisingtheSubject.html
2. Documents examined include government reports and papers, a database containing 1200 individual school project reports, theses and scholarly research publications examining aspects of this reform project.
3. To be approved, the project proposals not only must be clearly organized with literature reviews, budgets, project plans, methods and 'improvement goals aligned with strategies and measures', but also must show baseline and improvement targets, ongoing administrative support, a project

coordinator, knowledge dissemination plan, and community/parent involvement (McEwan, 2008 p. 5).

4. Six organizations developed the AISI in 1999-2000: Alberta Education, Alberta Home and School Councils' Association (AHSCA), Alberta School Boards Association (ASBA), Alberta Teachers' Association (ATA), Association of School Business Officials of Alberta (ASBOA), and College of Alberta School Superintendents (CASS). In 2000, University Faculties of Education (Alberta, Calgary, Lethbridge) were also invited to join the partnership.

References

Alberta Education (2008) *AISI Facts*. Available at: http://education.alberta.ca/admin/aisi/about/whatisaisi.aspx (accessed 20 October 2008).

Alberta Learning (1999) *Framework for the Alberta Initiative for School Improvement*, Alberta Learning, Government of Alberta (Edmonton, AB, Alberta Education).

Alberta Learning (2004) *Improving Student Learning: Provincial Report for Cycle 1 (2000–2003)*. Available at: http://education.alberta.ca/media/325050/AnnReoprtFull_2001.pdf (accessed 20 October 2008).

Alberta Teachers Association (2008) Partnering for Success: The influence of AISI on Alberta's Faculties of Education, *ATA Magazine*, 85 (4). Available at: http://www.teachers.ab.ca/Quick%20Links/Publications/Magazine/Volume%2085/Number%204/Articles/Pages/Partnering%20for%20Success.aspx (accessed 20 October 2008).

Burger, J., Aitken, A., Brandon, J., Klinck, P., McKinnon, G. & Multch, S. (2001) The Next Generation of Basic Education Accountability in Alberta, Canada: A policy dialogue, *International Electronic Journal For Leadership in Learning*, 5:19. Available at: http://www.ucalgary.ca/iejll/burger_aitken_brandon_klinck_mckinnon_mutch (accessed 20 October 2008).

Bloomfield, B. & Vurdubakis, T. (1999) The Outer Limits: Monsters, actor networks and the writing of displacement, *Organization*, 6: 4, pp. 625–648.

Bowker, G. C. & Star, S.L. (2000) *Sorting Things Out: Classification and its consequences* (Cambridge, MA, MIT Press).

Busch, L. (1997) *Actor Networks and the Division of Knowledge in the University*. Paper presented at the annual meetings of the American Educational Research Association, Chicago, IL, pp. 1–7.

Callon, M. (1986) Some Elements in a Sociology of Translation: Domestication of the scallops and fishermen of St Brieuc Bay, in: J. Law (ed.), *Action, Belief and Power* (London, Routledge), pp. 196–233.

Carson, T. & Sumara, D. J. (eds) (1997) *Action Research as a Living Practice* (New York, Peter Lang).

Clarke, J. (2002) A New Kind of Symmetry: Actor–network theories and the new literacy studies, *Studies in the Education of Adults*, 34:2, pp. 107–122.

Cochran-Smith, M. & Lytle, S.L. (1999) The Teacher Research Movement: A decade later, *Educational Researcher*, 28: 7, pp. 15–25

Crossan, M.M., Lane, H.W. & White, R.E. (1999) An Organizational Learning Framework: from intuition to institution, *Academy of Management Review*, 24: 2, pp. 522–537.

Czarniawska, B. & Hernes, T. (2005) Constructing Macro Actors According to ANT, in: B. Czarniawska & T. Hernes (eds), *Actor-Network Theory and Organizing* (Copenhagen, Liber and Copenhagen Business School Press), pp. 7–14.

DuFour, R. & Eaker, R. (1998) *Professional Learning Communities at Work*. (Alexandria, VA, Association for Supervision and Curriculum Development (ASCD).

Fenwick, T. & Edwards, R. (2010) *Actor Network Theory and Education* (London, Routledge).

Fullan, M. (1993) *Change Forces: Probing the depth of educational reform* (London, Routledge).

Hassard, J., Law J. & Lee, N. (1999) Introduction: Actor-network theory and managerialism, *Organization*, 6: 3, pp. 387–91.

Hetherington, K. & Law, J. (2000) After Networks: Guest editorial, *Environment and Planning D: Society and Space*, 18, pp. 127–132.

Judah, M-L. & Richardson, G. H. (2006) Between a Rock and a (Very) Hard Place: The ambiguous promise of action research in the context of state mandated teacher professional development, *Action Research*, 4:1, pp. 65–80.

Latour, B. (1996) *Aramis, or the Love of Technology* (Cambridge MA, Harvard University Press).

Law J. (1992) Notes on the Theory of the Actor Network: Ordering, strategy and heterogeneity, *Systematic Practice of Action Research*, 5:4, pp. 579–593.

Law, J. (1999) After Ant: Complexity, naming and topology, in: J. Hassard & J. Law (eds), *Actor Network Theory and After* (Oxford, Blackwell Publishers/The Sociological Review), pp. 1–14.

Law, J. (2003) *Ordering and Obduracy* (Lancaster, Centre for Science Studies, Lancaster University). Available at: http://www.comp.lancs.ac.uk/sociology/papers/Law-Ordering-and-Obduracy. pdf

Law, J. (2004) *After Method: Mess in social science research* (London, Routledge).

Law, J. & Hassard, J. (eds) (1999) *Actor Network Theory and After* (Oxford, Blackwell).

Lee, N. & Brown, S. (1994) Otherness and the Actor-Network: The undiscovered continent, *American Behavioural Scientist*, 37:6, pp. 772–90.

Luck, J. T. (2008) *Lost in Translations: A socio-technical study of interactive videoconferencing at an Australian university*. Unpublished doctoral thesis, Central Queensland University, Australia.

McEwan, N. (2008) *AISI—Seven Years of Enthusiasm: Improving learning and schools—innovation, renewal, sustainability*, Alberta Learning, Government of Alberta (Edmonton, AB, Alberta Education).

McLean, C. & Hassard, J. (2004) Symmetrical Absences/Symmetrical Absurdity: critical notes on the production of actor-network accounts, *Journal of Management Studies*, 41:3, pp. 493–519.

Mol, A. & Law, J. (1994) Regions, Networks and Fluids: Anaemia and social topology, *Social Studies of Science*, 24, pp. 641–671.

Nespor, J. (1994) *Knowledge in Motion: Space, time and curriculum in undergraduate physics and management* (London, Routledge).

Nespor, J. (2002) Networks and Contexts of Reform, *Journal of Educational Change*, 3, pp. 365–382.

Parsons, J., McRae, P., Taylor, L. with Larons, N. & Servage, L. (2006) *Celebrating School Improvement: Six lessons learned from Alberta's AISI projects* (Edmonton, Alberta, School Improvement Press).

Reeves, D. B. (2005) *Execution: Transforming research into action*. Presentation at the annual joint conference of the College of Alberta School Superintendents and Alberta Education, April, Edmonton, AB.

Stelmach, B. L. (2004) Unlocking the Schoolhouse Doors: Institutional constraints on parent and community involvement in a school improvement initiative, *Canadian Journal of Educational Administration and Policy*, 31, pp. 1–13.

Taylor, A., Neu, N. & Peters, F. (2002) Technocratic Control and Financial Governance: A case study of two school districts, *Educational Management Administration Leadership*, 30:4, pp. 469–499.

Strathern, M. (1996) Cutting the Network, *Journal of the Royal Anthropological Institute*, 2, pp. 517–535.

Thrift, N. (2000) Afterwords, *Environment and Planning D: Society and Space*, 18, pp. 213–255.

Weick, K. E. & Quinn, R. E. (1999) Organizational Change and Development, *Annual Review of Psychology*, 50, pp. 361–86.

Index

Researching Education Through Actor-Network Theory, First Edition. Edited by Tara Fenwick and Richard Edwards.
Chapters © 2012 The Authors. Book compilation © 2012 Philosophy of Education Society of Australasia.